THE
POLITICAL CAMPAIGN
"HOW TO"
GUIDE

NOLAN CROUSE

◆ FriesenPress

Suite 300 - 990 Fort St
Victoria, BC, V8V 3K2
Canada

www.friesenpress.com

Copyright © 2021 by Nolan Crouse
First Edition — 2021

All rights reserved.

No part of this publication may be reproduced in any form, or by any means, electronic or mechanical, including photocopying, recording, or any information browsing, storage, or retrieval system, without permission in writing from FriesenPress.

ISBN
978-1-03-911462-3 (Hardcover)
978-1-03-911461-6 (Paperback)
978-1-03-911463-0 (eBook)

1. Political Science, Political Process, Elections

Distributed to the trade by The Ingram Book Company

TABLE OF CONTENTS

ACKNOWLEDGEMENTS I

INTRODUCTION III

CHAPTER 1 - PREPARATION 1

    1.1 The epiphany 1

    1.2 Why serve 3

    1.3 When to begin 4

    1.4 What questions to ask 7

    1.5 What to "book" early 8

    1.6 Gathering intelligence and interviews 9

    1.7 Data gathering 11

    1.8 The database 13

    1.9 What the issues are 13

    1.10 The to-do list 16

    1.11 The "1,000" rule 16

CHAPTER 2 - THE GUIDING COALITION, TEAMS AND THE ARMY OF SUPPORT 19

    2.1 Successful campaigns 19

    2.2 Lists of contacts and supporters 21

    2.3 Core team 22

    2.4 Sub-teams 23

    2.5 Elected officials currently in office 24

    2.6 Community leaders 25

    2.7 Service groups and organizations 26

    2.8 Volunteers 26

2.9　Financial donors...28

　　2.10　Gifts in-kind donors..30

　　2.11　The many coalitions..30

　　2.12　Lawn sign hosts...32

　　2.13　The many whom you have forgotten about......................34

　　2.14　Invitations on election day and night..........................35

CHAPTER 3 - CAMPAIGN MESSAGING AND STRATEGY........................39

　　3.1　Candidate strengths..39

　　3.2　Candidate weaknesses and vulnerabilities.......................40

　　3.3　What we look for in leaders......................................41

　　3.4　Ethics, honesty and the message.................................41

　　3.5　Researching the opposition.......................................42

　　3.6　Opposition strengths, weaknesses and vulnerabilities............43

　　3.7　Current issues...43

　　3.8　Message and platform...44

　　3.9　Target audience (the voters).....................................46

　　3.10　Going high and going low..48

　　3.11　Emotional messaging...49

CHAPTER 4 - DEFINING "SELF"...51

　　4.1　Brand...51

　　4.2　Image...54

　　4.3　Colours...55

　　4.4　Photography...56

　　4.5　Logo..57

　　4.6　Slogan or tagline..58

　　4.7　Online image and presence.......................................59

　　4.8　Social media, blogging and the website..........................60

　　4.9　What not to do..62

CHAPTER 5 - BUDGET, SPENDING AND FUNDRAISING 63

    5.1 Why people give... 63

    5.2 Who to ask... 64

    5.3 Who asks 64

    5.4 Budget.. 65

    5.5 Keeping a database 66

    5.6 Fundraising ideas and tactics 67

    5.7 Banking... 68

    5.8 The myths 69

    5.9 Online 70

    5.10 Consistency with the laws....................................... 70

    5.11 Direct mail success..71

    5.12 The direct ask 71

    5.13 What not to do... 72

CHAPTER 6 - THE CAMPAIGN PLAN AND TACTICS 73

    6.1 The 7 P's of planning 73

    6.2 The tactics.. 73

    6.3 Assigning responsibilities....................................... 74

    6.4 The launch 75

    6.5 The factors that all add up 78

    6.6 Subsequent rallies or events 79

CHAPTER 7 - THE MESSAGE DELIVERY 81

    7.1 The profile of the voter 81

    7.2 Mailing materials.. 83

    7.3 Radio 83

    7.4 Television... 84

    7.5 Newspapers... 84

    7.6 Magazines 88

    7.7 Forums and public speaking opportunities....................... 89

    7.8 Emails 91

7.9	Website 91
7.10	Facebook 92
7.11	Twitter, Instagram and other 94
7.12	LinkedIn 94
7.13	Letters to the editor or columns 95
7.14	Door drops 96
7.15	Phoning 98
7.16	Robocalls and texting 99
7.17	Press releases 99
7.18	Google and YouTube 100
7.19	Informal venues 100
7.20	Blogs, recordings and podcasts 102
7.21	Lawn signs 102
7.22	Street signs 104
7.23	Lawn sign and street sign design 105
7.24	Billboards 108
7.25	Campaign office 108
7.26	Other visuals and infrastructure 109

CHAPTER 8 - DOOR KNOCKING 111

- 8.1 Impact and preparation 111
- 8.2 Image 115
- 8.3 Maps 116
- 8.4 Team 116
- 8.5 Tactics 117
- 8.6 Pace 120
- 8.7 Data collection 121
- 8.8 Tracking 122
- 8.9 Door knocking stories 123

CHAPTER 9 - THE COVID LESSONS 127

- 9.1 The game changed forever 127

THE POLITICAL CAMPAIGN "HOW-TO" GUIDE

    9.2 Door knocking 127

    9.3 Mail-in ballots 128

    9.4 Advanced voting. 128

    9.5 Virtual meetings 129

    9.6 Electronic voting. 129

CHAPTER 10 - DETAILS GET YOU TO ELECTION DAY 131

    10.1 The to-do list 131

    10.2 The naysayers 131

    10.3 Treatment of other candidates 133

    10.4 Treatment of non-voters 133

    10.5 You just don't know who.…. 134

    10.6 Just when you thought you had it all figured out 135

    10.7 The days (months) before you are officially a candidate 136

    10.8 The day of and day after becoming an official candidate 137

    10.9 Election Day 138

    10.10 The day after Election Day 140

    10.11 The days after election day 140

APPENDICES 143

    A. Announcement – actual word for word 143

    B. Speech at a Television Debate – actual word for word 144

    C. Post-Election Lawn Sign Instructions – actual word for word. 146

    D. Sample Speech – actual word for word 146

    E. Post-Election Thank You – actual word for word in

    the local newspaper 150

    F. Letter to Donors – actual word for word 151

ACKNOWLEDGEMENTS

THE POLITICAL CAMPAIGN "HOW-TO" GUIDE IS A labour of work that was made possible by the knowledge gained through observing, researching, reading about and experiencing several election campaigns during my years before running for office and as an elected official. During my various journeys to serve in public office for several terms, I was assisted by influential people such as former Mayor Anita Ratchinsky, former Mayor Paul Chalifoux, Campaign Manager Chuck Mulholland, and Member of Parliament Rob Merrifield. They were amongst many who guided me before or during these various journeys.

My immediate family were cheerleaders, deliverers of brochures and did whatever it took to simply get the jobs done during campaigns. My wife, Gwen, was supportive of my endeavour from the day I surprised her with my epiphany moment of "I am going to run" through to the time when we both knew it was time for me to leave the elected office world. The job of seeking, serving and writing about this experience has demonstrated to me that elected office is not a job for everyone. As such, I am in debt to her for her support throughout. My adult children (Curtis, Celina and Dalen) observed and helped with absolutely whatever was asked of them, as did so many of my friends, neighbours and relatives when I was seeking election and serving in office. I am deeply grateful to all of them.

Of all those who assisted me in this writing, I am particularly thankful to Debbie Anderson, my publishing consultant with FriesenPress who emailed me with encouragement when I needed it. To those who assisted with advice and proofreading, in particular Edith Martin and Sandy Clark who I turned to for proofreading.

I miss my mom and dad, and my sister Ann and brother Marvin, who would be proud knowing that I took this task on. Ann did some research for me, and that was deeply appreciated. My sister Sheila is supportive in all I do and always has been all of my life. To my children, Curtis, Celina and Dalen, I am forever grateful to you for helping me through life's journey.

It is said that "amateurs may write for their own amusement," but this is not an effort in amusement. This is a book which describes the rewards, fun and tough sledding of campaigning. It is also a thank you to many who assisted me in my journey in life, most of whom are complete strangers to me. They are called the voters.

In this book I hope to provide something that can assist others – serving to help others. The tips, checklists, insights and stories are amongst many ideas shared within to assist you in your journey to public office.

INTRODUCTION

"DO YOU WANT TO WIN?"

"Yes."

"What are you doing differently today than you were doing yesterday to demonstrate that?"

"Not sure."

"Then you don't want to win."

I was considering running for public office in an upcoming election.

My wakeup call was delivered in a 15-minute meeting with the Canadian Member of Parliament Rob Merrifield at his constituency office in Whitecourt, Alberta in the summer of 2004. I had reached out to meet with him, although he was a stranger to me, as I was beginning my due diligence to see if I was cut out to be in or interested in running for public office. He motivated me, encouraged me and also delivered the much-needed wake-up call questions that I quoted above as to my fence-sitting at the time of our meeting.

I was at a turning point in my working career and life. I had just sold a lumber business in Edmonton and was wrapping up my time as a hockey coach, general manager, league governor and junior hockey franchise co-owner. I had accomplished what I wanted to in industry and sport and was uncertain as to my next endeavour. I began searching what it would take to obtain my Master's degree. Our youngest son was in the United States at college, and our oldest two adult children were on their own. Like many at that stage in life, I searched for additional challenges and was seeking to "give back" even more than the giving we do when raising children.

Library searches, alternate career exploration and interviews with others were necessary to sort out what I wished to do next. I was not only seeking a path to elected office but also was considering other aspects of career planning.

I was also intent on growing a consulting business, which had some potential that I had not really explored much, but a long-time colleague and friend Brian McLeod owned a company called Panel Source International and he asked me to assist him in growing his wood-panel business. I was also a shareholder and assisting a company called Compaq Forestburg as its part-time chief operating officer, working to start up a new strawboard operation in east central Alberta. But I was not being fully utilized, nor was I fully satisfied with the work or path that I was undertaking.

Parallel to all this, I had come to know key members involved in the Chinese Ice Hockey Association during my time as junior coach of the Fort Saskatchewan Traders. The Chinese men's national ice hockey team, out of Harbin, China was seeking a Canadian coach to help bring a Canadian element to their national program. The agent that the hockey team had in place at the time wanted me to move to Harbin, China and assist them in their pursuit to move up the ladder of the world rankings, sitting in 30th place in the world ranking at the time.

During this time, one of the elected officials I met was our local Member of Parliament John Williams. After visiting him in his constituency office in St. Albert, I was impressed enough to decide to join the board of directors that governed the federal constituency that I lived in and for which he was the representative. Most of my interest was in learning something completely new. Indeed, I did not particularly care for politics but was willing to learn.

So, I had lots of irons in the fire and was working to keep them all hot, but "full of uncertainty" is mostly how I would describe the time. The more I began to understand the four orders of government in my community, the more interested I became in being an elected official.

An old boss of mine, Phil Latos, had run for a school board some 30 years earlier and lost. I did not understand what the school boards did but I had respected this boss, so it was intriguing to know that someone I knew could have been elected while doing other work parallel to that. The second order of government I reviewed was the local mayor and council, and that too seemed intriguing, yet I did not know their roles, nor did I know most of the individuals on council at the time. I did know one councillor named Penny Reeves. Penny was also involved with the St. Albert Merchants Junior B Hockey Club that I was coaching at the time; consequently, that was an easy connection for me to make to learn from.

As far as the provincial government, it seemed that I knew no one in that inner circle; therefore, I did little research into its existence. The fourth and most senior order of government seemed the most interesting – the member of parliament. I came to learn that the timing was not on my side because if I was going to become involved in any elected office, I was looking to act in 2004. There was no federal or provincial election scheduled for 2004. I did not consider the Canadian Senate at the time as a viable option for various reasons, mostly out of a complete lack of understanding, and because a senate election process did not exist.

A fifth order of government also exists in several regions of Canada, where the public elects its representative to serve on regional boards. These are primarily in Ontario and British Columbia. I will discuss more on this order of elected officials in a subsequent chapter. Another order was any aboriginal government, which I did not qualify for because I did not live on a First Nation land and did not have any aboriginal ancestry.

MP Rob Merrifield's advice rang in my ears. If I wanted to serve and if I wanted to win an election, I had to jump in and take it seriously. Passive involvement never was a trait of mine.

In late August 2004, I shared with my wife that I was going to seek elected office in the local election in about six weeks' time with the City of St. Albert, Alberta, as a city councillor.

She said: "You're going to do what? You hate politics."

So, this book is born more than 15 years later; after four times seeking elected office and four successful attempts. It is as close as you can get to a step-by-step guide to help you become an elected official.

Advice, wisdom, stories, checklists and more are included.

"Knock, knock."
"Who's there?"
"Hi, my name is Nolan Crouse. I am running in the upcoming election to serve as a city councillor."
"Hi Nolan, do you want to win?"

CHAPTER 1
PREPARATION

1.1 THE EPIPHANY

IN THE INTRODUCTION TO THIS BOOK, I spoke of the important messaging that Rob Merrifield, MP, shared with me with his succinct question, "Do you want to win?" The moment I heard that from him was my epiphany moment.

You too will have your own epiphany moment when something trips your trigger to take the plunge into searching for an elected role that fits your skills and desires. You may have the equally important epiphany when you choose to seek a change of order of office being sought or when you decide to re-seek the office that you have been serving in. Each of these times may be a trigger from a friend or a moment of desire or ego-seeking, which at the time accompanies the rush of success felt when making a political decision that helps others.

There may be a moment when you realize that you can supplement your income, a time when you meet another elected official who you respect or look up to. It may be when you become frustrated with your current politicians and you believe that you could do a better job than they do. It could be a moment where someone taps you on the shoulder, asking you to serve – or simply like me, the realization could occur when you are looking for a new challenge that keeps the juices flowing.

The epiphany that moved me perhaps fed into my competitive winning nature of trying to "win" an election. Some have asked me, "Why did you run?" My 14-year-old granddaughter, Carolyn MacDonald, asked that of me recently and I answered the way I have answered it many times in the past. "I actually ran to find a new path out of hockey and forest products, not solely just to find a new path to serve." I had served others over the years in industry and hockey, but I wanted to serve more in the community and finally discovered how to.

Once I answered the question "Do you want to win?" my path was clear. I registered to seek office, and then I prepared to win. The decision was like many we make in life. Once you decide, the rest is details.

Speaking of making key decisions, when I was about 25 years old, I went moose hunting with three friends. I was walking down an old gravel road on that hunting trip and a man in his 80s stopped his truck and asked me what I was doing. I told him I was out hunting with some buddies and I was just walking back to my vehicle. He said, "Jump in and I will give you a ride." As we drove along that old wilderness access road, the elderly man looked at me and said, "Young man, hunting is like life: when you pull the trigger, if you hit your target, the fun is all over. Just remember that in life." With that, he dropped me off at my truck, and hours later at dusk our hunting team bagged one of the biggest bull moose anyone could imagine. A stuck-in-the-muskeg vehicle, a dark forest, access only through a swamp, and a blown engine in one of our trucks were all signs that the fun was all over. It was the last time I hunted. The old man was right when it came to hunting, and it is also true in politics.

I recall a turning point came in my political career when, as a sitting councillor, my mayor at the time was His Worship Paul Chalifoux. Paul was a consummate professional and in my three years working with him, I observed in him what a true statesman behaved like. He reached out to me one day when we were at a planning retreat and shared that he was going to seek provincial office instead of re-seeking the mayor's chair and he thought that I might be a good replacement for him. His respect for me that moment was an endorsement that I appreciated immensely and told him so. He had taught me the appropriate comportment as a mayor and how to work well with neighbouring municipalities during difficult annexation challenges. He taught me the importance of political teamwork and how to work with an outstanding city manager at the time, Bill Holtby. I was no doubt ready and able, and the opportunity was handed to me by a mentor.

While there were many days that it was not fun being in a political role, on balance I had by far more fun days than not. But the old man's metaphor passed onto me while hunting still holds true in some sense. Being targeted on social media is one of those areas that is not fun, as an example. But I had far more fun days serving than difficult days.

Running for office my first time and re-running the second time were some of my most favourite experiences. The lure of the win was invigorating. The door knocking, the advertising and the fast pace of a campaign were exiting. More on these times are discussed throughout this book.

1.2 WHY SERVE

While I believe it was United States President Lyndon B. Johnson who shared the perspective, I was not able to obtain the exact quote, but the essence is something like this: Your only focus as an unelected wannabe is to become elected. You cannot govern from the outside and can only govern after you are elected. You have to get elected to influence public policy, so don't pretend you are elected until you are. This statement influenced me many times during my four campaign periods. In fact, the president's inference is often a reference to the many false statements made by those seeking to become elected. I hear statements and read promises made by many who are campaigning regularly. Those who are campaigning are often telling voters something that is perhaps misleading just to obtain someone's vote. They may be making promises that eventually they are not able to keep. The reality is, you will not be able to tell everyone what they want to hear, just to get their vote. Many voters see through that and will not vote for you when you make false promises.

Related to the president's perspective is a reminder from a friend of mine, Tom Thompson, who I served with in the 1980s when the City of Grande Prairie, Alberta was bidding to host the 1995 Canada Winter Games. He was the Bid Committee Chair, and he would always remind board members that the process of bidding to win the hosting rights of the games was a far different process than putting on the games. Similarly, the process of attempting to become elected to a political office is in stark contrast to actually governing.

Once you understand that igniting event or compelling reason to run for office, the details of the strategy can then be embarked upon. We always need to understand the "why" we are seeking office as it will help fuel the heart during your time in elected office. Once the deeply held reasons of "why" disappear, the heart beats differently.

While there are strategies, tactics and a long list of to-dos which are outlined in the subsequent chapters, it is the "why" that fuels the heart and nurtures the desire to succeed. For me, the excitement of something so different and unique fueled that next chapter in life. I knew that politics had minimal connection to the careers and passions of my past (forest products and hockey) but it was what I was looking for. I always knew that the "'why' eats 'how' for breakfast" and understanding the "why" inside your heart makes the tactical approaches more motivating to do. While understated, once the reasons for running for office are articulated, the rest is the management of details.

Some jurisdictions permit seeking and serving two independent offices concurrently. These opportunities are limited and before you look to pursue this, a candidate must check with the authorities plus the legislation. Running for a school board parallel to running for reeve or regional councillor in a community may be examples of that. Some candidates even register for a federal or provincial riding in more than one jurisdiction and that may be problematic, pending legislation. In some situations, a candidate may choose to hold onto their current elected official role while seeking another office at a different order. Again, in these instances there may be ethical or legal matters to be considered.

If one is seeking another order of government while governing a different order or while in a different jurisdiction, it is common to take a leave of absence from the office possibly to be vacated to avoid real or perceived conflict. These are considerations that authorities are usually able to answer locally, and if not, obtaining appropriate legal advice is suggested.

1.3 WHEN TO BEGIN

When and where to begin is always a question for election or re-election. A rule of thumb is to begin now on intelligence and knowledge gathering. That intelligence gathering may help you determine if you are going to proceed. Some of this research may seem daunting, invigorating or simply "not for me," but the more information that you gather, the more informed your decision will be.

One of the very first stops that one seeking office needs to make is to obtain information on all the legal requirements for the office one is wishing to serve. While the related websites may not be entirely up to date at the time of your epiphany, it is critical that you obtain the most relevant information possible. There are specific requirements for all orders of government, First Nations, aboriginal councils, provinces, school boards, regions and municipalities that will vary. Therefore, research is necessary.

There are various acts throughout Canada that are to be adhered to throughout any election process for the various offices. The following is by no means a comprehensive list and is fairly generic given that each municipality, region, territory, province, First Nation or treaty area will have more specific information that is relevant. This list changes regularly. Each of these acts are usually readily found online and answers to any questions associated with the latest version are usually accessible by purchasing the latest version through the Queen's Printer in your jurisdiction. There may also be various regulations that support the relevant acts with additional supporting details.

The following are some examples:
- Canada Elections Act
- Constitution Act, 1867
- Parliament of Canada Act

- Various Métis Nations' acts in Canada
- Alberta Senate Election Act
- Various provincial elections acts in Canada
- Various municipal elections acts
- Various provincial election finances acts
- Various school act across Canada
- Various acts specific to some cities
- Various local government election act
- Various First Nations Elections acts across Canada

There are a number of critical websites you can look at, depending upon the order of government being pursued.

Websites may include the following:
- Elections Canada Website
- First Nations Websites
- Métis Nation Websites
- Aboriginal Websites
- Provincial Elections Websites
- Territorial Websites
- Municipal Websites
- School Board Websites
- Regional Elections Websites

For a member of parliament, a member of a provincial and territorial jurisdiction, or a member of a local government there may also be a specific website dedicated to the needs of that region or ward.

While financial disclosure requirements may or may not be easily available on the website, financial tracking is a critical practice that you must carry out from the minute that you begin the process. A simple Excel spreadsheet, a Scribbler or Word document may be adequate to begin with. Do not underestimate the importance of tracking every penny spent, kilometres driven, items donated to you and money raised throughout all aspects of this process, even before becoming an official candidate. You can determine at a later date how or if detailed financial matters are recorded and what qualifies as a legitimate expense, revenue or gift in kind.

One of the most forward thinking, gracious and true politicians I knew was a retired high school teacher, Len Bracko, whom I had the opportunity to serve with. He served as a city councillor and as a provincial member of the Legislative Assembly of Alberta and also sought an elected senator-in-waiting seat in Alberta. When I first announced that I was running for the first time, I learned that Len was also running as an incumbent and was one of my competitors for six vacancies. Len reached out to me and asked if we could meet at a Tim Hortons. It was at that moment that I was taught three important lessons that I have never forgotten, and those lessons assisted me in further election campaigns.

When we sat down at Tim Hortons, Len, a stranger to me, had with him a huge rolled-up map of the city where we were both running for council. It was a map of every street, every house and every house address – something that I did not know even existed. He gave it to me and said it was his gift to me to help me win a seat. There were 21 candidates seeking six seats and he had 21 of these maps printed at the cost of three dollars each and gave each of his competitors a map. The first lesson he taught in that moment was simple: "know your community." The second lesson was "door knock, and here is a map to go by." The third lesson was one that was a political message (Len was the master) and it was "I am helping you." Len knew that eventually the word would spread that he was helping all his competitors, and some would team up with him and some would vote for him and some would spread the word that he was such a good person for doing such a good deed. This last lesson was that your competitors may be your biggest supporters, as each of those competitors has a voter following – treat them with respect and dignity and the word will spread. This is also true for any negative treatment. Those who disrespect others will be exposed.

Obtain a map, get to know your competitors and treat your competitors as friends.

There will be local rules, bylaws, handbooks, legislations, procedures, processes and protocols, some of which may not be available until very late in a campaign or election process. You need to learn where and from whom that material is to be obtained. There will be deadlines outlining when you can submit paperwork, when you are able to begin raising funds, when you are able to put up signs and more. The smaller communities in Canada do not have the resources to develop or distribute this information as readily or as early as the larger communities and knowing where to find what and when is critical for a candidate. Get to know the lay of the land when it comes to what is required, what is permitted and when.

Find someone who may be familiar with the previous election for that order of office and perhaps someone may have a copy of information (voter turnout, demographics, deadlines etc.) from a previous election. As stated, gathering intelligence and knowledge is vital. A local government authority will be able and willing to provide you with the best schedule information that is available at the time of your queries.

Make a list of people you wish to meet with, interview or gather intelligence from. Individuals from outside your community or outside the local jurisdiction are good people to meet with to reduce the probability of bias and to increase the likelihood of unfettered and frank input coming to you.

Obtain the local information as quickly as you can.

Where you begin is as follows:

1. Search for the relevant legislation
2. Search online for relevant intelligence
3. Begin early tracking of financials
4. Obtain relevant map(s)
5. Obtain relevant documents, past and current
6. Obtain schedule information
7. Reserve domain name(s) for your website
8. Create social media and email accounts

1.4 WHAT QUESTIONS TO ASK

In an article written and posted on her website (danikloo.com) by former municipal councillor and member of the legislative assembly candidate Danielle Klooster, she identifies five terrible reasons to run for office and lists them as follows:

1. "People are ready for change."
2. "I'm going to clean house."
3. "I'm going to fix 'xyz'."
4. "We've got to get rid of the current corrupt bunch."
5. "I'm going to lower your taxes."

This insight is valuable. Candidates often make promises and statements related to these five reasons and it is unwise to do so for numerous reasons. The key reason is that they may not be facts and may not be promises that you can keep.

During a campaign you may continue to struggle with whether to run or not. There are often as many struggles with ensuring the subsequent survival if elected, but each day the reasons to seek office (or not) become clearer once the research and work begins.

Think about what values you will hold dearly such that you can thrive and survive during and following the election. For example, following the election, I was most interested in providing leadership for a new recreation complex, and therefore I valued all input in this regard.

1.5 WHAT TO "BOOK" EARLY

There are some crucial first steps during an election process, possibly even before you have declared yourself as a candidate.

First of all, it is necessary for you to view your calendar differently during a campaign period than you might otherwise. "Do you want to win?" may mean that you need to postpone, reschedule, not attend or cancel events or matters that you may normally find important. Leaving the jurisdictional area for an overseas vacation is an obvious example of something to consider not doing, because you need to spend your time on the tactics in front of you. Celebrating birthdays or anniversaries, going on shopping trips, attending your favourite concert or participating in sporting events are activities that may need to become discretionary or delayed for a while. Consider your calendar as more of a public calendar for a period of time. Someone running in a federal election as a member of parliament, running to be premier or seeking the mayor's chair in a major city will certainly need to approach this differently than someone running for council in a small village in Canada. The principle remains, however, that your calendar needs to be heavily scrutinized if you want to win.

An additional consideration to be discussed later is that an incumbent may be required to address matters of importance, regardless of the campaign timing. Depending on the order of government or circumstances, the business of governing may not stop just because of the election campaign period, but the discretionary use of the calendar changes. It changes both ethically and administratively and may even change legally depending on the rules relative to the candidate's declaration or writ of a particular circumstance.

A candidate who is contemplating running should consider what to book early as part of a "critical path" of decisions. The jurisdiction and the order of government will influence the critical list as to what to plan, book, raise funds for or spend funds on. For example, at the municipal level for a village of 500, the requirements are much different than for a city of 500,000 people.

School board campaign planning is different than aboriginal, municipal, provincial, territorial or federal campaign planning, but there are some things that all candidates should consider.

1. Billboards are expensive and are often pre-booked by others months in advance of an election day. Therefore, it is one of the earliest matters to consider if you plan to use billboards.
2. Booking of your lawn sign manufacturer is another key decision to make early as there will be lead time and backlog for sign manufacturing.

3. Ordering of signage stakes (wire or wooden) should be taken care of because their supply and demand is cyclical with elections.
4. Office space for short-term campaign needs is often difficult to attain and landlords are reluctant to lease to candidates for only a few weeks. If you are planning on renting a campaign office, book the location as soon as you can.
5. The gathering location for Election Day and election night for family, friends, volunteers and supporters needs to be booked in advance. These locations in most communities are abundant, but there are usually some choice locations that get booked quickly by the candidates who are planning ahead, by insiders or by those who have the funds raised to do so.
6. Book the prime spots in the media. For example, the inside of the front page of a newspaper or prime time on radio and television needs to be booked, and perhaps partially paid for early.

While there are other critical elements of the critical path, these matters need to be completed early. Book early and cancel later if not needed or if you decide not to run.

1.6 GATHERING INTELLIGENCE AND INTERVIEWS

An internationally renowned change management expert, John Kotter, teaches that there are some key elements required during times of making change. Running for office and making change have some similarities because some of one's life will change if elected. Schedule, public scrutiny and visibility are only some of the things that may change if elected. What Kotter teaches is that it is important prior to embarking on change of any sort that there is intelligence and data gathering. The amount of effort in making this change to becoming an elected official will need to be commensurate with the intelligence gathered, information found and data collected.

It is important to collect the information covering legal, jurisdictional and financial requirements. Those are the areas needing to be understood well enough to keep you on the right path. It helps keep you out of trouble when you are unsure if you are following the rules of the road. But there is also the anecdotal intelligence and interviews that can help you get insight into some of the approaches and wisdom of others who have experienced the road to either failure or success.

While discussing with others the concept of running or re-running for elected office will cause speculation and rumours, it is more important that you collect the intelligence than it is to keep everything secret. Find others that you can confide in to give you unfiltered, candid commentary and advice. You recall that I chose to meet with a member of parliament who served outside my jurisdiction. I did that twice. Once I met with MP David Chatters, a gracious and popular man who had experienced several federal elections. He assisted me, along with MP Rob Merrifield, with insight. Because I was no "threat" to either of them as I was not trying to take their jobs, they were willing to be open and to share.

Similarly, with members of the legislature of a territory or province, or a band councillor, if you can get a phone interview, virtual or face-to-face meeting with someone outside your constituency, that non-threatening and unfiltered advice may be the best advice that you can obtain.

Additionally, gather intelligence from those to whose incumbency you are of no threat . Make contact with those who served, and make contact with those who were successful in their election bids. Interview others who were not successful in their election bids. Well-known Canadian governance author, consultant and speaker George Cuff was more than willing to give me three or four hours of his time over lunch, mentoring me and providing advice as to what to do and what not to do. He was a former elected official with great insight.

When I first contemplated running for municipal council, I first reached out to two elected officials whom I knew. One was Doug Ritzen, a lawyer and hockey dad whom I had come to know. He was serving on council at the time. He gave me the cold, hard facts about what I was facing. He was not running again and was willing to be bold, honest and forthright.

I also reached out to a councilwoman named Penny Reeves who had served on a city council for several terms and had been defeated as an incumbent over a controversial issue. Since I had known her through hockey, she was more than willing to invite me to her home. I heard from both her and her husband about what to do and what not to do, about campaigning and what to expect once elected.

Interviews and intelligence gathering from individuals who have walked a mile in the shoes is critical. I was a sponge for knowledge and intelligence and befriending and interviewing others during the process. Asking for help and advice is a strength and not a weakness.

Ask those you can confide in, those who know you, or those who will be frank with you the following questions, and take note of their answers. The questions to ask are these: "If I were to run for public office, what would be my Achilles heels? What am I not good at? What will others exploit or criticize or not like about me? In other words, what things about me would cause someone not to vote for me?" This frank feedback allows you to strategize accordingly.

On a related note, while I was the mayor of St. Albert, I once attended a luncheon to support women wishing to seek political office in the City of Edmonton. It was a lunch of about 100 women plus a handful of men, all there to support the need to have more women become elected to office. Two women were introduced as candidates who were seeking to be elected to vacant seats in that upcoming City of Edmonton municipal election. I privately introduced myself to each of them during the luncheon and gave them each a business card. One of the two women gave me her email address and I reached out to her after that lunch, offering to help. She did not reply. Neither of the two candidates reached back to see if I had any advice after my 13 years being on council. I would have openly shared insight and advice. Neither of the two candidates got elected.

1.7 DATA GATHERING

Understanding the local jurisdiction is crucial to determine many matters such as what is important to the voters, what geographic areas to campaign in, what issues there are to learn about, what the demographics are, and what the regional and local politics look like.

For some jurisdictions, there are municipal wards, councillor surgeries, council wards or regions that have websites for the needs of that specific area of a municipality, school jurisdiction or region.

Members of parliament and members of provincial and territorial constituencies or jurisdictions may also have websites dedicated to candidate needs.

In some provinces where there is an upper tier of municipal government providing regional services, it is important that you gather the particular intelligence and rules that are required for that specific tier, which may be called a county, a regional county municipality, a regional municipality or a regional district. Some governments that have regional entities in Nova Scotia, Alberta and Quebec may be administered as though they are a single municipality, a specialized municipality or a regional county municipality. It requires detailed research to understand the specific requirements for each circumstance. For example, three municipalities in Nova Scotia are designated as a regional municipality covering an entire region which includes formerly incorporated towns, villages and even cities. In Alberta there are six similar jurisdictions that are called specialized municipalities.

The types of municipal governments in Canada are different from province to province and a candidate should understand the structure so as to know the issues, the types of voters and where the voters reside. Historically, the smallest governments are called towns, villages, townships, hamlets and even parishes. In some provinces hamlets are not incorporated, while in others they may be. The term borough may be familiar to some, but there are no longer any boroughs outside of Quebec. In Quebec, there is no legal distinction between cities and towns, and many across Canada will use the generic term "town" to describe an urban area of any size. In Quebec, a borough refers to an administrative division of a municipality and only eight municipalities there are divided into boroughs. A candidate must review these eight for any unique election requirements.

Some areas of Canada are actually not incorporated in that they do not have a municipal government at all. Government services in these unincorporated areas are provided by a local service district, a local services board, the province or the territory itself.

School boards may require a religious affiliation or language affiliation, which must be researched and understood.

Aboriginal communities in Canada such as band councils, First Nations and Métis settlements may have requirements of residency and running for chief or councillor will have unique conditions that requires research.

Provincial and territory information is readily available on each jurisdiction's website. Federal requirements are always available online as well.

The results of the previous election matters to some degree. Voter turnout, demographics and any other data that may give insight into a campaign strategy matters for you to obtain. For example, in all four elections that I ran in within my nearby neighbourhood of 8,000 residents, I fared much better than in areas of the city where others likely had never even visited the area where I lived. Schools, local sports, familiarity, ease of door knocking, biking routes, kids' friends, walking trails, neighbours and rumours all help with planning a strategy.

Candidates need to come to know the location of and approaches to accessing condominium developments, gated communities, seniors' lodges, apartments and more. There are likely laws that will assist or prohibit access to many of these sites.

Obtain the donor information that is public from previous elections' candidates. This data provides some intelligence as to who may be willing and able to support candidates or political parties. Names of corporations, donors, individuals and organizations that have already donated to others are all helpful to one raising campaign funds.

In summary:
1. Gather data from your jurisdiction
2. Gather historical election results data
3. Obtain statistics

1.8 THE DATABASE

Begin building a database for several aspects. If you have a board of directors already in place, someone would likely be willing to volunteer and research the data that is already available. Such boards are more common for federal, provincial and territorial jurisdictions but less so for aboriginal, school board, regional and local elections.

Prepare database spreadsheets on areas that are important, which may include the following:

1. Volunteers
2. Friends
3. Relatives
4. Neighbours
5. Potential corporate donors
6. Potential individual donors
7. Media outlets
8. Lawn or yard sign hosts
9. School boards
10. Not-for-profits
11. Budget
12. Donation tracking
13. Thank-you list
14. Expenses
15. Travel and mileage log
16. Ideas and their sources
17. Mailing addresses
18. Email addresses
19. Door knocking locations
20. Flyer distribution tracking
21. Donors not to contact
22. Households not to contact
23. Businesses and business owners/managers
24. Community and union leaders

1.9 WHAT THE ISSUES ARE

While the issues matter, taking a position on some issues may or may not matter. Allow me to open with this.

When I was door knocking, I was asked many times, "What is your position on the non-smoking bylaw?" In that particular case, because it was an election issue, I felt I needed to take a black-and-white stance and stand behind it, regardless of the consequences at the ballot box. I could have stated, "If elected, I will look at all sides and make my best educated decision." That is usually the best answer in most circumstances. Remember Lyndon B. Johnson's advice: since you are not governing just yet, you have to find ways to get into office first. But when it came to smoking and no-smoking, I already had a position and decided to always state it.

One election we were faced with a plebiscite as to whether we would construct a new recreation centre. I was often asked on forums, in the media and during door knocking what my position was, and I always told others, "I do plan to vote yes on the plebiscite myself, but if elected, I will respect the wishes of the results of the plebiscite."

During one election, a very controversial decision about one particular road was needed. It was the very first election that I had run in and I asked my wife if she knew anything about this road. We got the street map out and went for a walk. I recall standing in the middle of a wheat field, looking at where this road was penciled in. My wife knew more about it than I did, but it was I who was having to answer questions. On issues you might not be sure about, it is easiest to take the high road and reverse the question if asked. I would state, "I am not sure, so tell me what you think," or "If I am elected, I will learn as much as I can and make an informed decision at that time, because I don't know right now."

It is those candidates who take a position on every topic asked who then find themselves expected to follow through on what they told others. Worse yet, you may be on the fence for all kinds of reasons on some matters and you tell one person one thing and another person another thing because you are not certain. Telling people what they want to hear may help you accomplish what you are seeking (to get a vote), but it may undermine your credibility because in the next election or during your time in office, that same person or group may recall (or publicize) your previous opinion.

I coached a hockey player, Doug Lemieux, before he became a successful businessman. His father, Roger Lemieux, became an elected colleague of mine one election and successfully returned for a second term on City Council. When I looked at his election brochure there were no platform issues stated, just a picture of his family and his dog and a few generic character statements about how trustworthy he was. When I asked him why he did not take a position on key topics, he stated, "I can only promise that I will work hard and be honest. I cannot promise anything else, because I don't know enough about any issue." He got elected based on being known as a businessperson, based on integrity, based on the beautiful photo on his simple brochure, and he avoided any form of controversy for all six years in office. I teased him one time that he got elected with nothing on his brochure, and his response was, "I'll not be wrong that way."

Usually, campaign periods come and go quite quickly. In partisan politics where there is often a known platform published by someone other than the candidate, what position a candidate must take is spelled out more clearly, and one is usually expected to tow the party line once elected. Certainly, that will preclude many good candidates from becoming elected because Canadians will most often vote along party lines. However, in most other elections in Canada, partisanship is less prevalent, and more flexibility is afforded candidates who are not beholden to the higher-ranking elected leader.

In British Columbia and in other parts of Canada, some municipal candidates will declare which party they are affiliated with as it allows voters to know the general bent of their policy views. I phoned one mayoral candidate who had been acclaimed in British Columbia but had also declared his party affiliation. He also publicly named which councillors he supported to influence who voters should vote for. I called and asked his thoughts on the dangers of publicly supporting councillors who were seeking to serve on his council. He told me if he were to do it over again, he would have stayed silent. The councillor candidates he was supporting did not get elected and those who he publicly did not support did get elected. He caused himself grief for four years.

Voter turnout percentages can actually influence the issues, but it may not be easily linked. A ballot question or plebiscite on an important topic will drive voter turnout up and the turnouts vary from order to order of government. Federal election turnout has declined over the decades and in recent elections, turnout is 60%-70%, while provincial and territorial turnout is more variable and in Canada may range from 40%-80% depending on many factors. The local election turnout for council members ranges from 15%-50% across Canada.

Based on Brock University research conducted in 2008, the primary reasons for not voting in Canadian elections are one, lack of interest or apathy; two, negativity toward candidates; and three, personal (such as being too busy or due to illness). Voting station questioning of voters or actual voting problems were also cited often as reasons for not voting.

For local elections, lack of interest is cited as the main reason why people do not vote, and this is in part because those closest to the people are the locally elected officials. Locally elected officials are seen by Canadians as the most responsive to voters' needs compared to other orders of government; therefore, the electorate ends up being mostly satisfied with their local governments and may not turn out to vote in the local school board or council member elections.

A key role for a candidate's preparation is to help get the electorate or voter interested in what the candidate is interested in and vice versa.

1.10 THE TO-DO LIST

Every idea may gain you a vote. It may be the vote you needed. Keep a master list of those ideas and where they came from. An election campaign is a series of to-dos, and you will perhaps have many supporters helping with the to-dos. Keep a master list of the input, the "aha" moments and the information you gain while contemplating running and while running for office. Each idea may be possible to be acted upon by you, your family, a volunteer or a stranger wishing to help.

Comprehensive to-do lists are within the chapters of this book and may trigger some additional ideas that you can apply to your own campaign.

1.11 THE "1,000" RULE

During my intelligence gathering process, I decided to reach out to someone who was a former mayor whom I had not met, Anita Ratchinsky. I phoned her and she shared something that was quite telling and an "aha" moment to assist me. She shared that in a city of 60,000, I need to know or know of 1,000 people. She said this translated into possibly 3,000 highly likely votes and it was important in order to become successful in getting elected to office. That 1,000 represented about 2% of the population in my community. The relative scale certainly changes depending on the size of community, but that was her rule of thumb that she gave to others who asked for her advice. In a community of less than 1,000, seeking office will mean that if you know or know of most residents, your chance of success at the ballot box is remarkably high. It may seem daunting that you need to have a relationship with 1,000 residents, but nevertheless her advice was important. The 1,000-person advice was useful in helping me with the work that I undertook following that bit of intelligence.

In most communities one cannot easily answer how many people one knows or knows of, but I thought I would take the challenge seriously from the former mayor. Out came the white pages book, a ruler and a highlighter. I went through the 25,000-line items in that phone book over a several-hour period and stopped at every name for a split second. Soon the highlighter was busy. There were neighbours, and there were the parents of my three children's school friends. There were folks from church, schoolteachers and babysitters. There were football parents, hockey contacts, my wife's curling team members and more. There were not-for-profit leaders, store owners and simply people I had forgotten about. I discovered individuals whom I knew but who I did not know had moved to the community. I also did a count as to the number of relatives that I actually had in town.

Access to a white pages listing is not as easy as it once was, but there are many other techniques to determine who may live in your community, many of whom that you had lost touch with. Reverse lookup by streets, check your photo albums and review class pictures from your children and the boards of many of the churches and not-for-profits in your community. The work that you put into this name gathering will pay dividends because it is that group who will rally voters for you, volunteer with you, encourage others to help or simply vote for you. It is that group who will put up a lawn sign or put a sign in their window supporting you. It is that group who will donate gifts in kind, time and money. It is those who know you who will be important to helping you become elected.

There is a voter registry available sometimes in some communities or in some constituencies that is obtained legally and ethically depending on the order of government and the laws that are in place for obtaining that information. The registry is confidential in most jurisdictions.

Once you have had your epiphany, once you have completed all your due diligence, once you have collected data, once you have reached a level of comfort in moving to the next phase, the excitement of a potential run to seek office will become evident. If you remain unsure, if you believe elected office is not for you, or if you have too much anxiety about the process or the possibility of winning or losing, continue to interview, assess, research and turn over the rocks to see what might be right for you. If it is right, play to win. If it is not right, have no regrets.

When to disclose your plan to the entire electorate or public is an entirely separate strategy that has a political impact that will be discussed in a subsequent chapter.

Assuming you have decided to run, it is game on!

CHAPTER 2
THE GUIDING COALITION, TEAMS AND THE ARMY OF SUPPORT

2.1 SUCCESSFUL CAMPAIGNS

IT HAS BEEN SAID BY MANY IN various aspects of life, "I am the captain of my ship and master of my fate." Nothing holds this statement truer than when it comes to the importance of a candidate in charge of their own campaign. It takes a lot of help to become elected, and yet it is critical for someone to lead the parade.

Successful campaigns ensure that the candidate, or the party leader is out front and indeed is the centerpiece of any campaign. This is not always the case for some campaigns, and that is a mistake. At times a campaign manager or communications team member attempts to deliver a message or answer a question at a door that the candidate should deliver or certainly approve of. Equally, at times, messaging and candidate branding is misunderstood by campaign workers when the volunteers are simply working to the best of their ability and eager to help someone along the way.

I have interviewed several successful and unsuccessful election candidates, read six books on the subject and observed several election processes. I spent countless hours in the library and online reviewing past election results, and I have spoken with countless people about the processes required to win.

While there is apathy toward politics, I am 100% convinced there are eight common themes to winning an election.

They are as follows:
1. People need to have heard your name or have seen your name a lot.

2. Studies have shown that a person who knows you is worth 10 to 50 votes. This data speaks to campaigns in Canada where the number of eligible voters is greater than 10,000 for the office that you are seeking. If 1,000 people know you (or claim to know you), that may be enough to win an election, because each of them influences 10 others. Your family and your closest friends influence 50 others. Appeal to them to help you!
3. Network to beat heck and do it yourself as well as with your team.
4. Door knocking is key to success at every level of government across Canada in every community, bar none. This is the secret (and it is real fun) to a successful campaign.
5. Have a team of 6 to 10 individuals who will closely help you, and that usually means about 100 are actually assisting in some fashion, some even unknowingly. Keep the top leadership team tight and small. You must be in control of decisions and your brand along the way.
6. Play to win, don't play to compete. Do it for 90 days, 5:00 a.m. to 11:00 p.m.
7. Generally, final vote results are proportional to the amount of spending on a campaign (on ads, signs, etc.). You may not need money, but it helps a lot. Issues are not always important. YOU are important and selling yourself matters more than having answers to the issues.
8. In partisan politics, it is critical that the candidates follow the party leader, follow the mantra, follow the branding and live and die by that approach.

I have learned from all the books I read, from all the interviews and from those who got elected that **from a style point of view,** the following are important:

1. Know the key issues. Have a general position, but market yourself first, the issues second. If you do not have a position on an issue, ask the voter what their opinion is or state that you need to listen to all viewpoints.
2. Don't be afraid to ask for advice on issues and market yourself.
3. Don't be afraid to say, "I don't know" and market yourself.
4. Be your own spokesperson. Address your own (or your party's) platform. This is your campaign; be in control as it is you (or your party) the voters are voting for.
5. Emotional campaigning works – showing that you care. Demand better if trying to unseat an opponent, offer solutions

positively and offer solutions delivered passionately rather than mudslinging.

When it comes to being the candidate of choice at the federal or provincial levels, first there is the requirement to become the nominee through a nomination process. That process is about three basic factors:

1. Rallying a large team who are solely focused on selling memberships.
2. Ensuring your large team of salespeople actually are selling memberships to support your nomination.
3. Getting those members who purchased a membership to actually get out and vote for you at your nomination election.

The nomination process is an entirely different process than the process is once you are nominated.

2.2 LISTS OF CONTACTS AND SUPPORTERS

A key aspect of any short-term initiative is that there are regular communication channels to those who are helping. Whether that be in business, government, volunteering or a not-for-profit, respecting the communication needs that others have is paramount to success. Nothing holds truer during an election campaign. Usually, campaigns are a sprint, not a marathon, and while some of the largest campaigns at the national level and some at the provincial level may last an entire year, most campaigns will be compressed into a 3-to-12-week timeframe. Approximately 50% of all candidates at all levels are incumbents and are obligated to continue to govern and therefore may dedicate little time or resources toward any campaign effort until a short time before an election. When it comes to the contacts and supporters, however, the candidate needs to ensure these lists of contacts and supporters are maintained by someone. Communicating your intent and plans to the supporters will assist in rallying a team around your campaign efforts.

I recall in my first campaign, since I decided so late that I was going to seek office, I had recruited no one to assist and when I did reach out to some, many were already committed to helping others because I was so late in contacting them. Of course, no one even knew that I was contemplating a run. Giving people late notice can make it difficult to recruit volunteers. I was able to find a good team, however, and it was fun.

All that said, the minute that you decide you are going to simply kick tires, or the minute that you decide you are going to run, you must begin making a list. This is when you should begin using one of your spreadsheets, adding names as you think of them. Later in this chapter there is a memory-jogger list to perhaps make you think of the many whom you have forgotten about but who may become your most avid supporters, volunteers and ultimately those who vote for you.

Begin your list early and create a spreadsheet, and as you obtain or think about phone numbers, email addresses, street addresses or mailing addresses, expand this list. It will be remarkably valuable for weeks and even years.

2.3 CORE TEAM

The core team of one's campaign team depends upon many factors. The size of the constituency, the budget, the level of office and the size of the community are only a few factors of consideration.

Suffice it to say that in the smallest of communities in Canada, where the population is only 500 like in Irma, Alberta, the campaign structure is remarkably different than in a large, diverse area such as the Halifax Regional Municipality in Nova Scotia that is widely spread out with almost 450,000 residents.

The structure is different for a Métis settlement than it is for Inuit or for the more than 600 First Nations in Canada compared to a municipality.

The structure is also substantially different for a member of parliament riding in Nunavut of 32,000 residents, widely dispersed over the territory, when compared to a riding such as in Niagara Falls, Ontario where the area is densely populated with 130,000 residents. Similarly, there may be differences where federal ridings are highly contested with a history of close elections compared to some where the outcome has been consistently predictable for many consecutive elections. Provincially, the same holds true in a constituency where an incumbent premier is vulnerable and may have a substantially different campaign team than one where polling is showing a landslide for a long-time popular incumbent candidate.

There are some common considerations for most federal, provincial, territorial, regional, aboriginal, school board and municipal elections, however, and those will be covered here.

Since there are so many combinations of an organization chart, because there is such a wide variety of campaigns, you will need to think about the types of roles that you wish to fill and what degree of complexity or simplicity you wish to have in your own chart. For example, a candidate may require an independent financial agent, regardless of the situation. Family may play a key role in your campaign. Regardless of how big or small your family is, their understanding and support goes a long way to helping you succeed.

Most successful campaigns have a core team of 5 to 10 people who are leading the sub-teams. There are six members who should be on all teams, and it is my belief that all campaigns should include the candidate. In some federal and provincial ridings and campaigns, the candidate may not be readily available for meetings but must be available to discuss any matter of question or confusion at all times.

Ecanvasser has recapped and posted online their lessons learned in evaluating over 500 campaigns, and their three key themes were that all campaigns need to have the following:

1. strong organization and coordination,
2. door knocking efficiency, and
3. quality canvassing.

In Canada, any election core team should include:

- Candidate
- Campaign manager
- Door knocking coordinator
- Volunteer coordinator
- Financial manager/agent
- Signage coordinator

2.4 SUB-TEAMS

I have determined that there are about 65 factors, each weighted differently, that go into the evaluation by the public as to whether to vote for a particular candidate or not. In highly partisan politics the weighting of some of those 65 factors are so significant that it is nearly impossible for all of the other factors combined to overcome the significance of party affiliation. That said, one must put together the teams that reflect some of these factors. While not all these 65 factors are listed here, each of them are discussed in one form or another in this book, some at length and some briefly.

The size of the campaign, the riding, the region, the municipality or the jurisdiction may determine to what degree these sub-teams are populated, if at all, with named volunteers (or paid personnel if appropriate).

The following are categories that volunteers can be assigned to when forming sub-teams. Each category represents what the volunteers would be responsible for.

- Traditional media
- Nomination administration
- Campaign office

- Photography
- Brochures
- Scheduling
- Street signs
- Lawn signs
- Website maintenance
- Door knocking
- Social media
- Debates
- Communications
- Volunteers
- Election Day and night
- Election day voter turnout
- Scrutineers
- Quality canvassing

2.5 ELECTED OFFICIALS CURRENTLY IN OFFICE

Many incumbents are very coy or private about their intent to re-run for their seat for various reasons. First of all, those currently in office must continue to govern and should not spend any resources or time that may even be illegal or unethical, be in conflict with the office they are in, or in conflict with the staff they are currently working with. This is a mistake that is made by some and is often closely scrutinized and noticed by members of the public or media.

Second, incumbents have an advantage of being able to capture attention by the sheer nature of their role and consequently are usually able to be in governing mode right up to the election. Again, there will be public and media scrutiny on what may appear to be campaigning and what may appear to be simply governing, so an incumbent must be sensitive to such challenges while still governing in office.

Third, it may be advantageous for an incumbent to maintain the privacy of their decision in order to thwart or delay a competitor's strategy and fundraising.

Fourth, the incumbent may be attempting to keep their team, who are still actively governing, focused on the work they are undertaking during their time in office. Any election announcement that comes too early may cause fractionation to occur within the team and may also lead to distraction of any number of the incumbents.

A fifth reason incumbents do not disclose is that they may be putting all their strategies in place to announce, to recruit volunteers, to plan their campaign and to fundraise in an attempt to be more organized than any competitor.

Sixth, an incumbent's immediate colleague may be poised to campaign against the incumbent and may make mistakes in tactics if the incumbent changes course unexpectedly. Like in a game of poker, if someone shows their hand too early or too late, the other person(s) may be able to take advantage.

Seventh, incumbents may be seen as lame ducks after they announce their intent to not re-seek office. Their leadership comes into question and they may even postpone difficult government decisions, leaving those decisions to the next governing body, because advancing controversial or difficult matters may not be possible during a sensitive election time frame.

This is why paying attention to the incumbent's behaviour is important, but it is often impossible to tell what an incumbent's intentions may be, especially with the experienced incumbents.

Finally, on this matter, one must remember that Canadians are very forgiving of mistakes and even inappropriate behaviours when it comes to their elected officials, unless something lingers or is egregious. As such, the incumbent gets a lot of free passes for past errors. Our memories are short, a lot of change takes place between election cycles and the voter coming to the polling booth is usually judging based on a fairly short-term body of work by an incumbent. "What have you done for me lately?" is a question that comes to mind when people cast their vote.

2.6 COMMUNITY LEADERS

Earlier I stated that studies show that a person who knows you is worth 10 to 50 votes by their connection to others. If that person is a non-family community leader and is openly endorsing you, many voters will follow that lead. Open endorsements on social media, brochures, websites, radio, television and newspapers are all ways that help drive that number from 10 to 50.

That leader offering an endorsement may be a political leader, business leader, philanthropist, professional or a well-known not-for-profit leader. If you know a community leader well enough to ask for an endorsement statement from them, you should do just that. The "no" you already have, so the "yes" you have to ask for from that person. Elections are political and this is a form of politics that is legitimate and powerful.

If it is possible to have a community leader as a key person on your campaign team, especially in one of those key 5 to 10 roles, the word will spread, and that impact may multiply past the 50 that I referred to.

2.7 SERVICE GROUPS AND ORGANIZATIONS

People vote, not organizations.

People vote, not businesses.

While this is understood on the surface, it is wise for campaign strategies at all orders of office to value both these sectors. People own businesses, people volunteer and people govern organizations of all kinds. While there may be a small number of organizations from which one would need to keep a distance, for the most part support of these two broad sectors can only help a candidate. As a candidate, if elected, you will represent the individuals involved in these organizations. Addressing the importance of business and economic prosperity is never wrong. Supporting those involved in volunteering for service clubs, sports organizations, arts organizations and many other groups is never wrong. Since some of these groups may have an initiative that they wish to have addressed during the campaign such as business taxes, or development, or a new shiny asset in your community, making campaign promises to any specific interest group is unwise. Since you are representing all people, all views will eventually matter, and offering support for interest groups is important, but offering any commitment is potentially harmful to your election success or subsequent re-election if you are not able to follow through on election promises.

2.8 VOLUNTEERS

Most, if not all Canadian campaigns at all levels and in all orders of government rely on some volunteerism. Even in the smallest of election jurisdictions, someone is likely volunteering to perform administration, signing of documents or providing third-party oversight for financial disclosures. Of course, there are examples where the candidate does everything and are acclaimed and no volunteer effort is needed, but for the purpose of this book, let us assume that volunteerism is occurring.

Volunteers must be recruited, valued, recognized, thanked and treated as a full-fledged team member working to get the candidate elected. Candidates (or a designated team member) must keep a spreadsheet of all the names, what support they volunteered for, their contact information and any specific data that is important to communication and follow-up. For many campaigns, volunteers simply wish to offer their lawn to host a lawn sign, while some volunteers are prepared to work full time because they believe in the candidate, the cause or the party that the candidate is running for.

Many volunteers enjoy the challenge, and Election Day may even be an anticlimactic moment for them. Many volunteers yearn to be around others.

Being part of a team is invigorating and important regardless of the candidate's views or party affiliation. Some volunteers join to make a change of their representative from one party or individual to another. Others join a team to learn about how to actually run a campaign because of their interest in doing so someday themselves. I recall when I was considering running, I chose to join a team to learn about the plan. I attended one meeting before advising the individual who I was assisting that I was actually considering running myself, and therefore I declined attending any further meetings.

There are also those who join campaigns to gather intelligence for another, opposing campaign. While this is not common, this nefarious approach is one of many reasons why campaigns can be nasty and one of the reasons elected officials (as a general category) are not well-trusted.

One of the key portfolios for your campaign team needs to include coordinating of volunteers. It is surprising the number of volunteers who come out "of the woodwork" to volunteer to assist, when they may be virtual strangers to the candidate.

Finally, it is critical for many reasons, not the least of which is future election volunteer needs, that a list of volunteers is kept so that appropriate thank-you messages can be sent following the election period. Win or lose, an appropriate thank you of a gift, a phone call or a card is important regardless of the volunteer's contribution.

I volunteered to work on the campaign for a candidate once. Both my wife and I donated funds. I helped with many aspects of the campaign, including attending meetings, posting on social media and providing endorsements. When the campaign ended, there was no thank you, no card, no text and no email of any sort whatsoever. It was a major failure of that campaign. Other volunteers on the campaign team voiced similar disappointment in this regard. It also ensured that I would not volunteer for any future elections for that person.

Figure 1. *Volunteer list*

	Name (last)	Name (first)	#	Street Address	Phone #	email	Thanks sent	Other
1	Anderson	Jan	33	Rayond Street	555-444-2222	Jan@jananderson.com	Yes	Helped with signs
2	Babiuk	Jill	45	Super Road	555-444-2229	Jil@jillwebsite.com	No	Was a lawn sign host
3	Chinook	Robert	6	Area Red	555-444-2345	Bchinook@chinook.ca	No	Treasurer
4	Doots	Dick	7	Subway Drive	555-444-4567	dick@doots.ca	No	Campaign Manager
5	Everson	James	9	Axel Street	555-444-9999	everson@jamese.ca	No	Brochure drop
6	Fairmont	Fred	8	Ham Crescent	555-444-2221	fredfair@fredfair.com	No	Door knocking help
7								
8								
9								
10								
11								
12								
13								
14								
15								
16								

2.9 FINANCIAL DONORS

Most campaigns require some funding.

When I was seeking election once, Jerry Naqvi, the owner of a major development company (Cameron Development Corporation) asked to meet me for lunch. Jerry is a gracious man whom I had not met before. He wanted to get to know me and get to know my thoughts about development in our community. As it turns out, his company later became extremely important for the growth of the community, but at the time when I met with him the company had no holdings in the city. After lunch that day, he pushed a piece of paper across the table toward me, folded, and as I looked at it, I could tell it was a cheque, filled in with a donation amount. I did not notice how much it was but thanked him for the donation as he mentioned that campaigns are expensive and he was prepared to assist. I recall mentioning to him that I did not know what I would ever do in return. This statement was a rather naïve view on my part, and he knew it, but he stated, "In life sometimes you need to just give a penny and someday the penny comes back and sometimes it does not, but you still need to give the penny." I never forgot that, and it is how many people view donating to an election campaign. There cannot be a quid pro quo for donations, and those who give and take on that premise are unwise to do so.

Donors who donate cash should donate because they believe in a cause, a platform, the party or the candidate. Donating or accepting for favours is unethical. It is not uncommon for some elected officials to actually return funds to the donor so that they do not feel beholden to anyone or to anything.

This is also the reason why so many elected officials at the local level (municipal, aboriginal, and school boards) self-fund their own campaigns. This is much easier to do in the smallest jurisdictions in Canada and less so in partisan politics; it is difficult to do for many candidates in larger jurisdictions.

Any campaign that accepts cash donations must form a bank account and it is wise to have two signatures on that account so that there is accountability for the handling of the money. The other reason is so that accountability can be maintained for the reporting of finances to the governing body that oversees the election financing process for the election being administered.

In the previous chapter, a list of possible spreadsheets was provided. Donor listing is one of those spreadsheets mentioned, and it is critical that all money raised is included in that spreadsheet. For some, donors may claim the donation as a tax deduction, and for everyone involved, all paper trails need to match and add up. This is an area that the public, media, the governing oversight agency, other candidates (losing candidates) will often view after an election, looking for irregularities that may intentionally or unintentionally occur.

Figure 2. *Contributors*

	Name	Address	City	Code	Donation	Letter	Thanks Sent
1	Ally Homes	#200 - 4th Steet	Edmonton, AB	T5H 3B8	$100.00	Yes	Yes
2	Bobs Plumbing	88 Down Street	St. Albert, AB	T8N 6K9	$25.00	Yes	No
3	Raelene Jank	999 Curve Avenue	Edmonton, AB	T5S 1J8	Lumber	Yes	No
4							
5							
6							
7							
8							
9							
10							
11							
12							
13							
14							
15							
16							
	Total				$125.00		

Finally, and perhaps the most important matter relative to receiving cash contributions, the laws of the land must be strictly adhered to and the legislation that governs that matter must be reviewed and followed to the letter. The legislation across Canada varies from order to order of government. The legislation may be different from one jurisdiction to another if there are local policies that may be more stringent than the higher order of governing bodies. Corporate donations, reporting timeframes, donation limits, random cash donations and leftover funds are all examples of matters requiring a plan and oversight.

Finally, of course, do not forget the importance of the thank-you process for any donation received.

2.10 GIFTS IN-KIND DONORS

Many donors donate gifts in kind, and like cash donations, a comprehensive listing must be maintained for all the same reasons as for cash donations. Equally, the laws must be followed when receiving gifts in kind contributions. The legislation that governs gifts in kind must be reviewed, and yet its application may be more ambiguous than with cash donations (e.g., in-kind donations could be mileage, food, office supplies, etc.). Again, the legislation across Canada varies from order to order of government and the legislation may be different from one jurisdiction to another. There may also be local policies that are more stringent than the policies of the higher order of government. Corporate donations of food, election signage, print materials and office space are all matters requiring a tracking plan and oversight. The donations of incidentals are often overlooked and thought by many to be gestures similar to volunteering, but the importance of tracking and adhering to the legislation remains critical.

Another spreadsheet!

Another thank-you card!

Another item for your financial experts to assist you with.

2.11 THE MANY COALITIONS

"A rising tide lifts all ships" is a saying that holds true in political campaigns.

This is particularly true in partisan or party politics. During an election process, all members (or most) of one party or of one ideology align themselves with one platform or one manifesto. In these instances, voters will tend to vote for the party, the leader of that party or the ideology that the leader is espousing. Some voters may support a candidate who is not in alignment with their political ideology out of loyalty to that person. Over the long haul, however, party politics wins the day, and the candidate must understand that the bias that voters have comes out when they are privately casting their vote inside the voting booth. Supporting someone publicly does not mean the voter will vote for that person privately.

For non-partisan elections, one approach that is often used (and used with success) is when more than one candidate links to an important issue or to someone else who is also on the same ballot. This approach may work when two or three candidates may wish to be seen as a coalition and they secure each other's supporters' votes. This is an example of "a rising tide lifts all ships" where all voters vote for the same group because of what that group, represented by the pairs of candidates, believes in.

It is also common for voters to look for candidate groupings who align on issues. For example, perhaps a voter is prepared to vote for everyone who is in favour of a new swimming pool and looks for candidates who have boldly stated their support for that pool. There are numerous examples of that across Canada. Candidates may gamble on what side the majority of voters will be on and hitch their election success to that wagon. For candidates to hitch their success to electing three or four as a block or slate will often be viewed by the voting public as a degree of collusion and will usually thereby be rejected.

All that said, reach out to all candidates who are on a ballot. To your competition, be kind, wish them luck, obtain their email addresses and phone numbers so that you can stay in touch. You may need each other before the election date and perhaps even more so on the night of the election. Obtain their website addresses and scour them. Obtain all their social media information and follow them and befriend them on all these sites. Ask them to follow you if you will follow them. Spread the word with others that you are being kind and considerate; the word of your kindness will spread. Late in the evening and at nighttime, you may assist them in driving traffic to their website or social media accounts. You should find appropriate positive things to say to and about them. All this positive dialogue disarms any negative that may be targeted toward you. None of this may seem natural or instinctively wise. Trust me, it is wise. A rising tide lifts your ship too.

Figure 3. *Contact information of all candidates*

	Name	Email Addresses	Cell Numbers	Office
	All Candidates for all election openings Election 2000			
1	Bobby Jones	bobby@bobbyjones.com	555-555-8888	Mayor
2	Cathy James	cathy@cathyjames.com	555-555-7777	Councillor
3	Janie Jackson	janie@janiejackson.com	555-555-6666	School
4				
5				
6				
7				
8				
9				
10				
11				
12				
13				
14				
15				
16				

2.12 LAWN SIGN HOSTS

This category of need is one of the most time consuming and mileage-intensive parts of anyone's campaign. In a later chapter I will discuss street signs and other related signage.

Lawn signs are believed to be quite significant to demonstrating support for a candidate. Endorsement by a resident with a sign in their yard will no doubt be viewed by others in the neighbourhood or those driving by.

There are several aspects to lawn signs that should be considered, as each aspect is critical.

1. Have no fear in asking someone if you can post a lawn sign in their yard somewhere. (The worst that they can say is "no.")
2. Have one person responsible to oversee this initiative to ensure that there is consistency and discipline to the plan.
3. Arrange the number of drivers necessary to volunteer to accomplish this task. (Having 25 lawn signs hosted around a rural community is remarkably different than having 200.)
4. Know the exact address or directions to find the location. (Putting a lawn sign on the lawn or driveway of someone who did not request one is a common mistake.)

THE POLITICAL CAMPAIGN "HOW-TO" GUIDE

5. Put the lawn sign in a conspicuous place and facing the direction in which it will be most visible. It is wise to have printing on both sides of lawn signs so that traffic traveling from either direction are able to view the sign.
6. Place the sign away from foot traffic so that passers-by do not trample, steal or otherwise vandalize the sign.
7. Place the sign in a location that does not require any inappropriate trampling of sod, flower beds or gardens.
8. Place the sign in a spot where there is no risk to underground infrastructure when stakes are used (e.g., plastic sprinklers or water shut-off valves).
9. Place instructions in the mailbox or at a location near the sign as to what to do with the sign upon completion of the election. Options may be to toss it in the garbage, recycle it, leave it leaning in a conspicuous spot for pickup or keep it until the next election. (In one community, a group of volunteers from a service club volunteered to drive all over the community picking up all the signs for candidates on the understanding that the candidates would donate funds to that service club.)

Another spreadsheet.
Another thank-you opportunity.

Figure 4. *Lawn sign hosts*

Lawn Signs

	Name (last)	Name (first)	#	Street Address	Phone #	email	Thanks sent	Information
1	Anderson	Jan	33	Rayond Street	555-444-2222	Jan@jananderson.com	No	Sideyard only
2	Babiuk	Jill	45	Super Road	555-444-2229	Jil@jillwebsite.com	No	On back fence
3	Chinook	Robert	6	Area Red	555-444-2345	Bchinook@chinook.ca	Yes	Front yard by tree
4	Doots	Dick	7	Subway Drive	555-444-4567	dick@doots.ca	Yes	Not before October 1
5	Everson	James	9	Axel Street	555-444-9999	everson@jamese.ca	Yes	Lean by garage
6	Fairmont	Fred	8	Ham Crescent	555-444-2221	fredfair@fredfair.com	Yes	Need 4 signs
7								
8								
9								
10								
11								
12								
13								
14								
15								
16								

2.13 THE MANY WHOM YOU HAVE FORGOTTEN ABOUT

Those who support you will come from all walks of life. There will be friends, neighbours, relatives and strangers. One simply does not know from whom or why the support comes forth, but as you look to obtain support for volunteers, scrutineers, lawn sign hosts or simply voters, support may come from any number of categories or groups.

This list may serve as a memory jogger for you to consider who to reach out to.

The "Memory Jogger" list; the many whom you have forgotten about:

- Friends
- Over 80
- Under 20
- Acquaintances
- Families with children
- Families who adopted
- Single moms
- Single dads
- Salespeople
- Coaches
- Teachers
- Classmates
- Special needs
- Soccer
- Hockey
- Ringette
- Karate
- Lacrosse
- Baseball
- Curling
- Bowling
- Hobbyists
- Your favourite sport
- Your spouse's favourite sport
- Your son's favourite sport
- Phone contacts
- Children's friends
- Children's friends' parents
- Store clerks
- Bank tellers
- Business owners
- Waiters
- Former neighbours
- Former employees
- Former co-workers
- Who your sister knows
- Who your brother knows
- Who other family members know
- Card players
- Campers
- School graduating class
- Workout colleagues
- Smilers
- Bald people
- Shift workers
- Postal workers
- Comedians
- Fishers
- Christmas card givers
- Photographers

- Your daughter's favourite sport
- Parent teacher association
- LGBTQ community
- Apartment dwellers
- Condominium dwellers
- Places of worship
- Faith leaders
- Facebook friends
- Doctors
- Chiropractors
- New parents
- Vacationers
- Seniors
- Seniors' lodges
- Engineers
- Truck drivers
- Carpenters
- Handy-people
- Thrifty individuals
- Skiers
- Snowboarders
- Skateboarders
- Scouts
- Guides
- Spouse's friends
- Employee assistants
- Boards of directors
- Bearded people
- Security personnel
- Ethnic groups
- In-laws
- Wedding party
- Transit workers and users
- Pharmacists
- Lawyers
- Accountants
- Dry cleaners
- Auto mechanics
- Daycare workers
- Snowbirds
- Email contacts
- Bosses
- Other candidates
- Musicians
- Choir or other singers
- Friends of all ethnicities
- Universities
- Service clubs
- Twitter followers
- Instagram followers

Each one of these may trigger an emotion, a memory or story that will assist you in making contact with someone along your journey to Election Day.

2.14 INVITATIONS ON ELECTION DAY AND NIGHT

You will need to plan for the election day and night with the belief that you will win a seat, and most importantly to gather and acknowledge those who assisted you in the journey. Plan this sooner rather than later.

The campaign gathering may be at a home, at a community hall or church. It may be at a hotel or any number of rental location options.

A key principle on election night is to invite more people rather than less. This is worth explaining. If it is known that two campaign teams are joining together to have an election night celebration or volunteer gathering, the two candidates' teams begin to support each other's candidates at the ballot box as well. Such a plan exudes teamwork and collaboration. If the venue has the capacity to host more than one campaign team, the benefits of many attendees far outweigh any downside that may be thought of. It may even be common for one candidate to be successful in the election and another not so. Some volunteers and candidates will simply be appreciative and find their way home quite quickly after the election results are known.

The number of real election volunteer "junkies" is far fewer than is on a candidate's list. Many individuals are willing to support and help, but fewer are interested in joining an evening of political celebration or disappointment. Most volunteers stay at home and await results to be communicated to them; after all, they also have busy lives.

While there is potentially a significant expense to inviting more volunteers than less, there are ideas that can offset the cost of thanking those who were part of the overall effort. It is also important that all financial laws be followed and that the costs and revenues of the celebration day are recorded.

Costs may be offset by some of the following ideas:

- Ask for the day and evening to be a potluck. Volunteers understand this and are more than willing to assist in this regard.
- Have a cash bar, with non-alcoholic beverages available for purchase.
- Ask others to bring their own refreshments, as long as the venue permits such.
- Join with other candidates and split the cost and any generated revenue.
- Ask the management or ownership of the venue to forgive some of the costs as an election expense.
- Offer a donation opportunity. While some may be willing to donate, all laws must be adhered to.

Here are some considerations for who to invite:

- School boards candidates or representatives
- Municipal candidates or representatives
- Media
- Provincial candidates or representatives
- Member of parliament candidates or representatives
- Competitors
- Other elected officials from other orders of governing bodies

- Donors
- Volunteers

Election night itself is an opportunity for perhaps another spreadsheet. You may not be able to invite everyone or many due to cost or logistics, so this is certainly a key consideration. Again, invite as many as you can or can afford to.

Another thank-you card.

Another item for your financial experts to assist you with.

CHAPTER 3
CAMPAIGN MESSAGING AND STRATEGY

3.1 CANDIDATE STRENGTHS

CANDIDATES MUST KNOW WHO THEY ARE AND who they are not. They must know their own strengths, weaknesses and vulnerabilities. Frank perspectives from others who know you is important because we do not always see ourselves as others see us.

It could be said for political campaigns:

"Play to your strengths."
"Go with what brung ya."

There are many approaches to the human side of a campaign strategy, but there is one element that matters the most, and that is authenticity. It is the easiest to describe, the easiest to be when speaking and it is the easiest way to be when in front of others such as the media or when door knocking. As such, your starting point will need to be playing to your strengths, and this is what you do well. If you are an accountant, a trucker or a restaurant worker, each career and each experience can be exploited to assist in developing your platform. A university student may speak about the importance of education, while an engineer may speak to the importance of infrastructure and a stay-at-home mom may speak about the importance of family and community. Each career and experience is who you are and therefore allows you to "go with what brung ya." For example, in my first campaign I supported a new recreation centre because I knew recreation well and could defend and speak to it at any time.

As you develop a media strategy (to be covered in a later chapter), you will need to deepen your brand and your communication plan around those strengths. Others may work to exploit your weaknesses, but you are able to exploit your strengths, and it is equally one of the reasons why your volunteers are drawn to you.

Consider strengths in all sorts of categories. If you have served on a board, you have governance knowledge. If you have coached a youth sports team, you have demonstrated leadership and teamwork skills.

Even a perceived weakness may be seen by some as a strength. As an example, you may be able to claim that you actually grew up in the area that you are wishing to serve in. Others may view you as not having diverse experiences because of that. Perhaps you have lived in several communities and therefore are able to describe experiences from outside the immediate community – ideas that you can bring to your current community. Others may see that as a weakness because you did not grow up in the area you are looking to serve in. There are many examples like this.

Strengths may be education, career, work or volunteer roles, gender, race, ethnicity, socioeconomic diversity, religion, business acumen, academic standing, charm, speaking ability, athleticism, age, multilingualism and even appearance. We are not able to easily ascertain why voters vote for a certain candidate. There are biases, prejudices and how we relate to others, and what others value are not always known or admitted by them. Playing to your strengths is important; however, flaunting a strength that may be seen as inappropriate will also be seen as unacceptable, even when someone may agree with you. For example, attempting to overvalue your education level may be inappropriate with some audiences. The matter is a very tender issue that requires the finesse of the best. This is why authenticity and tact are critically important.

3.2 CANDIDATE WEAKNESSES AND VULNERABILITIES

You will need to assess "who you are" using several approaches. Google yourself. Are there any inappropriate videos on YouTube? Check what you have stated on Twitter, check what is on your Instagram feed, your website and your Facebook pages. If there are matters of significant controversy, this can only be problematic at all levels. There may be matters that may assist you in becoming elected and which may equally cause you to not be voted for. Check all social media platforms. A Google history is nearly impossible to have changed, especially in the short term. Therefore, that history is critically important. Additionally, Google all other candidates seeking the same office that you are, as you can learn more about who your competitors are.

A second approach to self-assessment is to list your own weaknesses and consider a strategy to address that list. Consider a social media strategy or adding someone to your campaign team who can assist in countering the weaknesses that you know you have demonstrated. Asking your family for their perceptions of your weaknesses that could have election consequences is also important to helping you improve your campaign strategy. This is not always an easy exercise, but you have to answer the key question, "Do you want to win?"

A third strategy is to develop a list of the five questions that you do not want to get asked during a campaign period. Now, no one may ever ask those questions, but this exercise forces you to think about where your lack of knowledge may be or where your vulnerabilities are. These questions may be quite personal, and you would need to be able to answer them if asked at a forum, at a debate, on Twitter, in a radio interview, by email or by a television station. Practice these answers in front of others confidentially if you need to before facing the public.

You must have a plan to address your weaknesses, your vulnerabilities and where you can be exploited by others. This can be a personal strategy or one that you and your team construct together.

Finally, there may be some weaknesses that are showstoppers. Being unable to speak French when seeking office on a francophone school board or not being Catholic but running for a Catholic school board trustee may be showstoppers, and you will need to determine when that might be the case.

3.3 WHAT WE LOOK FOR IN LEADERS

We look for many attributes and skills in our leaders, and without a doubt, the electorate is seeking some or all of these following attributes in our elected leaders.

We look for leaders who

- model the way,
- inspire with a vision and are forward thinking,
- enable others to act,
- demonstrate the willingness to challenge the status quo,
- encourage the heart and are inspirational,
- demonstrate integrity and honesty, and
- are competent.

3.4 ETHICS, HONESTY AND THE MESSAGE

While I used the word authenticity when I spoke to playing to your strengths, there is no substitute for being ethical and honest beyond reproach. While many are not able to judge this aspect of a candidate when the candidate is first seeking office, it becomes more apparent by the time a candidate seeks office as an incumbent, after already serving for one or more terms. The brand, reputation and style become apparent over time and the public will usually pass judgment based on a series of events and circumstances that occur over the period between elections. For new candidates, it is harder for the general public to judge these attributes.

One example of something that has assisted me in my personal and professional life in this regard is carrying a tape recorder. I carry one with me everywhere, including in my vehicle, to remind me regularly of commitments I make. Whether it is to return phone calls, to email someone, to send someone birthday wishes or to meet a commitment made to others during a busy moment, I speak into my tape recorder those reminders. Not just with elected officials, but with life in general, we often say, "I will give you a call sometime", or "I will get back to you on that", or "let's grab a lunch and talk about that." It is incumbent on the elected official (the leader) to demonstrate meeting commitments. It is one thing to make that statement to a close friend, but in elected office, those phrases roll off the tongues of politicians day after day. Your voters, constituents, ratepayers and residents remember what you promised them or said to them, perhaps more than you may remember. So, keep notes, record commitments and follow up so that you are seen as someone who meets their commitments. When it comes time for re-election, the preferred brand for you is "he/she always does as he/she says" or "you can count on her/him." This deepens the trust that others have in you.

Finally, ensure that your materials, brochures, websites and other communication tools demonstrate the integrity of your messaging and the high standards that you demonstrate as a person. If your platform does nothing else, it needs to exude integrity, ethics and honesty. Hopefully, those traits are some of your strengths!

3.5 RESEARCHING THE OPPOSITION

Just as others will research you and your strengths, weaknesses and vulnerabilities, your own campaign has an equally important task to know about your competitors. Generally, Canadians are averse to negative campaigning, however, in recent years, it has become more and more common for negative campaigning and emotional appeal to be utilized. This approach is not reserved for short campaign periods, as opposing members of partisan politics spend years discrediting those who are governing and finding information damaging to the re-electability of the governing members. The media is more than happy to assist in reporting negative stories, as bad news travels well and all forms of traditional and social media are helpful in both positive and negative campaigning strategies.

You must be true to yourself in this regard. If you are comfortable with negative campaign approaches, it has proven to be successful. There is also a saying that "when you play with pigs, two things happen: the pig becomes happy, and both you and the pig gets dirty." Another saying is "when you lay down with dogs, you'll get up with fleas." While both these sayings are somewhat graphic, they do describe the potential of things not being "pretty" with negative campaigning. One who "lives in a glass house best not throw stones" is also an appropriate saying for this approach to seeking votes. So, if you plan to use negative campaigning strategies, understand that there are implications that may be difficult to work with.

No matter which approach you choose, you need to know your competitor. Another consideration is that many times candidates competing for the same level (school boards, city councils, etc.) often need to work together in the months or years ahead. Having bad blood between two community leaders is not something that is comfortable, and generally Canadians would prefer our leaders and candidates to offer solutions, ideas and positive change approaches instead of mudslinging. Mudslinging is often simply hurtful and not in the best interest of the public good.

3.6 OPPOSITION STRENGTHS, WEAKNESSES AND VULNERABILITIES

Once research is completed on the opposing candidates and their weaknesses, vulnerabilities and strengths are known, it is possible to develop a strategy that exploits their weaknesses if the opportunity presents itself. That strategy could be to run newspaper ads where you offer a solution that addresses a matter that you know is a weakness of a competitor. It may mean that at candidate public forums or during question-and-answer sessions you have planned a strategy that speaks to how someone else's vulnerability may play to your strengths. Knowing this intelligence matters at many levels as the public is often looking to draw contrast between two candidates. This is especially true for the undecided voter. In partisan politics, there are also many undecided voters who are seeking a home for their vote. For this reason, drawing contrast is critically important.

3.7 CURRENT ISSUES

Know the issues.

While character, integrity and authenticity of a candidate is front and centre for most voters, the candidates are expected to know the issues that are important to the voters. Voters expect the candidates to have opinions and expect candidates to be able to express those opinions. Voters look to candidates whose views align with their own views and will thereby possibly vote for that individual.

When it comes to party politics, candidates are generally expected to follow along the party lines as an overwhelming number of voters have deeply held beliefs that are along party lines. That loyalty is what candidates are expected to be beholden to, and while there are always exceptions to this rule, such is the case most of the time. Once an individual is named as a candidate for a particular party through the local nomination process, "towing the party line" is expected of them, and at times not following that party line may not even be tolerated by the party leadership. Many voters may not actually like a particular candidate and yet will hold their nose and vote for that same candidate because they represent the party or ideology that they themselves value. While there are some voters who vote for the candidate, it is usually the party that appeals to a partisan voter.

For aboriginal, school, regional, some territorial, and most municipal jurisdictions in Canada, the party or ideology influence is less prevalent. A candidate is expected to have a plank or platform to describe and to stand upon. That platform should have 3 to 10 elements to it and be able to be articulated by a candidate on a website, on a brochure or when knocking on doors. There are some municipal jurisdictions in Canada where party affiliations are actually stated by candidates running in these local elections.

It is advisable to have an "elevator speech," where you could articulate, in 30 seconds, the few matters that are important to you so that on the spur of the moment you are able to deliver that message to someone who is simply looking for brief descriptions or sound bites that matter to them.

During my first election campaign, as I went from door to door, I realized that the election issues on the voters' minds were only four issues, and while I could be evasive about one of those four, I was expected at the door to have a position on the other three and deliver that position succinctly in 30 seconds or less.

Know the key issues. Again, as mentioned earlier in the book, where you do not have knowledge or cannot take a stand, it is wise to say either "I do not know", or "What I can promise you is, if I am elected, I will learn as much as I can about that issue and all issues that I am faced with and I will make an informed decision." Voters are usually OK with that.

3.8 MESSAGE AND PLATFORM

With today's options for communications, there are multiple ways to distribute your message and platform, but it is critical to any election success that the public first know your name, in particular your last name. Let's face it, the ballots are populated with names and nothing else, and your name may be one of 2, 5, 10 or 30 names on a ballot. One differentiator will be the message and platform. Most importantly, the voters must be able to connect the name to the message. The voters must be able to first visualize the person, because for some, the name may matter even more than the message.

As the saying goes, "If a tree falls in a forest and no one is around to hear it, does it make a sound?" The same adage holds true for a political office candidate's messaging. If no one knows your name, who you are, what you stand for, or anything about you, they are less likely to vote for you than for someone they have become familiar with. The message or platform is an opportunity to deliver the information that voters seek. You may have a great message and great platform but if no one hears it or knows about it, it won't matter how good the platform is. Websites, social media, brochures, videos, mailouts, blogs, advertisements and emails are all examples of the approaches that you must consider using to communicate your name and message. For your campaign, you must answer the question about whether the tree that falls in the forest actually makes noise or not.

Earlier in the chapter, I stated that one of the things that voters look for in a leader is that they can "inspire with a vision and forward thinking." The most successful messaging is usually visionary and future thinking. Voters are seeking leaders who can see ahead and who have the leadership skills to improve the community, province, school, reserve, settlement, municipality, region, territory, riding or constituency that candidates are seeking to represent.

Candidates should also learn from others across Canada. Online, there are a tremendous number of ideas that websites may contain. It is relatively easy to find which jurisdictions have recently held elections (for all orders of government) and the current best approaches will generally be employed by many within those jurisdictions. For example, if Ontario recently held a provincial election, all the successful provincial candidates' websites are likely able to be viewed, and ideas can be gained by searching many of them. Similarly, if New Brunswick and Manitoba each had municipal elections, there may be numerous council member websites one can take ideas from. Greg Krischke, long time mayor of Leduc, Alberta explained to me, "This is called R&D, Rob and Duplicate." It works.

In another chapter, I will speak about the significance of the message and the platform in comparison to the many other elements of a successful election campaign.

3.9 TARGET AUDIENCE (THE VOTERS)

I had shared that based on some research by Ecanvasser of 500 campaigns, the key elements of successful campaigns are one, to have good organization structure; second, to have an efficient door knocking strategy; and third, to have quality canvassing for votes. Understanding the demographics, voter turnout and where to access your audience to maximize success in your campaign results matters. This is the type of research that can be done months in advance of your official campaign period and can even be an interesting research project for an early volunteer or for yourself.

Additionally, in provincial and federal ridings, there will be membership information, voting intelligence, turnout for various demographics and more. All of that past information may be critical to building the strategy to target the voting public in a way that maximizes voter turnout for a future election and specifically to target where your support may be the greatest.

There are many generalizations one may make, but suffice it to say that in Canada, the voter turnout percentage generally increases with age. For example, turnout of citizens over 65 years of age (seniors) for most elections is about 80%, while in the age range of 45 to 64 the turnout is closer to 70%. This is a reason why it is important for candidates to spend time in locations where seniors may be gathering or living. There are coffee shop gatherings, bridge clubs, seniors' lodges, seniors' sports and seniors' societies, just to name a few. Not only do seniors wish to be heard and respected, but senior citizens also wish to ensure there is a legacy for their families. Many seniors yearn to meet community leaders and influencers. It can also be said that this age group may have children and grandchildren whom they influence as to their voting preferences. Accordingly, part of any wise campaign strategy involves engaging in all sorts of activities where seniors are able to interact and communicate with prospective candidates.

Incumbents have a significant advantage over new candidates because of the incumbent's knowledge of the culture, connection with many of the seniors, name recognition and more. As such, incumbents are wise to maintain, and are usually comfortable having, good quality interactions with seniors.

There are many interactive opportunities that a candidate must seek and learn about. There are youth gatherings, markets, business gatherings and many events that take place that a potential candidate may wish to engage in over a period of time. Staying in the public realm and public view matters significantly.

There is another saying that "the world is run by those who show up," and it is certainly true in political office. If you are never seen, talked about or known for engaging with others, it is a challenge for voters to remember your name, your personality or to recall a visual of you when it comes time to select a candidate in the ballot box. Similarly, many candidates work on their community engagement or are heavily involved in their community for years prior to seeking any political office, and therefore, the public knowledge of them is much greater and their target voting audiences are more easily established. As an example, someone who served as a past chamber of commerce chair or library board chair for 10 years will be known very well in a community. The audience at the doors will be discussed in a later chapter, a strategy unto itself as the randomness of the voting audience increases when you ring a doorbell.

The canvassing strategy (one of the three major learnings from research by Ecanvasser) is even more of a critical aspect of elections where the membership is known or contact information is known and published to the candidates. Generally speaking, these are voters who have willingly provided their names and contact information, many knowing full well that they will be called or recruited to donate to, vote for or volunteer for a candidate. Making use of this information is essential for a candidate to win a party nomination race and is especially important to those who are running under a party banner. It is not uncommon for these voter lists to be held by someone from one election to the next and at times released earlier than permitted by law or policy. Over time, these lists often end up in the hands of many unethically because the value of contacting this "audience" is known by the seasoned election workers. Those who are guilty of this behaviour should be disqualified, because unfortunately this misuse of personal information is abused in Canada and certainly provides an unfair advantage for some candidates over others.

There may be any number of breakdowns of important blocks, groups or audiences that need to be assessed and which – depending on the position that you are seeking – will help determine which areas to invest more time in than others. For example, ethnic groups, church groups, youth, seniors, families or particular neighbourhoods may all be examples of where to target voters. Controversial development, economic development, environmental matters, social matters, day care issues, traffic issues, sports issues, arts issues, school concerns, university costs are some of many examples that may influence the audience that you are targeting mostly. Know the concern areas and know the areas where support is to be gained and plan your strategy accordingly.

Similarly, the platform that one runs on may dictate the audience that one spends more time nurturing, especially given that time is often short for any candidate seeking office. For example, if you are supporting the construction of a new road or a dog park, find those who agree with you to assist you in spreading the word.

3.10 GOING HIGH AND GOING LOW

You will need to determine what your campaign approach may be when raising the temperature of a campaign.

Remember, you are always trailing the leading candidate by one vote.

Never share with anyone that you are leading in any election. Bragging about polls will get you nowhere.

You should not share that you are the favourite to win, even if you believe that you are.

Take nothing for granted; expect it to be an uphill battle, as it usually is.

These above are simple examples of views that your communication tactics should be based upon. One comment made by a dear friend of mine, helped me understand what I was hearing from others when I ran for mayor one time. Brian McLeod, whom I had worked with and who was able to be frank with me stated, "In politics, people will tell you what you want to hear." He was so right, because person after person, door after door, meeting after meeting, people would say things like, "You've got my vote", or "I voted for you last time", or "You are better than the other person." It seemed like everyone was going to vote for me. I realized that the same was likely being said face to face with many of the other candidates seeking the same office that I was. It would only be a rare instance when someone would actually tell me face to face that they did not support me, something that could easily nurture a good conversation.

But determining whether to "go high or go low" certainly depends on many factors. If an opposing candidate is clearly vulnerable by some previous activity, it is important for the voting public to know about it. It may be done by a campaign advertising strategy, by leaked information to the media or by straight up confronting the matter by yourself. Perhaps someone on your campaign team may be the correct individual to ensure others are aware of it. My advice is to not go low for reasons discussed previously because you may simply get dirty playing in the mud.

During one election campaign, my son's rugby coach, Gareth Jones was running against 15 others seeking a chair on a council in the city we lived in. One of Gareth's 15 competitors knocked on Gareth's house door and Gareth's wife answered the door. The wife decided to play along and during the conversation the candidate at the door proceeded to tear apart Gareth after Gareth's wife asked the candidate, "What do you think of that guy Gareth Jones?" So, unbeknownst to this candidate, the wife obtained additional information. Over the next few weeks, she proceeded to spread the story to others about that door knocking experience and it no doubt contributed to Gareth Jones being elected and this other candidate not winning one of six vacant seats. In my opinion, going low hurt this candidate.

One does not know who is related to whom, who is friends with whom, who is a neighbour or who is an intimate partner! There are many connections that help us get elected and an equal number of connections that can ensure we do not capture someone's vote.

I ask the question, "What is the downside of going high?" and few can find an answer to that question. You can find the downside to going low, but seldom can you find a downside to going high. Whether it be in the media, at the door, in casual talk, or at public forums with many individuals, the benefits of going low are substantially less than the advantages of going and staying high.

Finally, like many other aspects of campaigning, if the candidate is able to stay above the fray of negative campaigning and not go low, there may be others on your team who can assist in ensuring the weaknesses and vulnerabilities of your opposing candidate(s) are known to the voting public. It is a fine line and important to think about. It may not be important to execute, but you need to be able to answer the basic question, "Do ya wanna win?" My younger sister, Ann, who did not live in my jurisdiction, obtained some information once on one of my competitors that I was reluctant to use, but it was fun to read about.

3.11 EMOTIONAL MESSAGING

It was shared with me once, "If you come across an elderly woman or man crying on the curb of a street and sit down beside that person, soon there will be two people possibly crying." This metaphor demonstrates that we relate to others when we feel emotion or find bonds and commonality.

It is proven through research that emotional messaging can have advantages and there are certainly tactics that allow this to be taken advantage of. Tugging at heart strings and having a personal touch with stories are two of many tactics that can assist a candidate in attaining support. Blogging may be an example of communicating these kinds of messages.

Emotional messaging may come from being photographed with your children, being with an elderly person or attending to the needs of others in a hospital. It may mean your brochure photo showcases your family pet or that your website shows you helping out at a food bank before or during a campaign period. You may choose to photograph your own parents as examples of support for older adults, thereby appealing to emotion.

Emotional messaging may also come in the form of a fiery campaign speech or challenging a competitor to a higher standard.

Certainly, there is a fine balance between going low or going high when it comes to your competitor, but nevertheless, finding emotional moments and situations clearly plays to a candidate's advantage.

Some of the most effective campaign strategies are those where one is allowed to "imagine" what is being described. If candidates are able to demonstrate the leadership skill of articulating a vision, with the emotional side of moving toward that vision, it is usually well received.

In the end, the candidate, whether they be an incumbent or a newbie to the table, each has to play to their strengths. As I stated earlier, you must go with what brought you to the place you are in. Others on your campaign team may be willing and able to do those things that you might not be able to do. If you are not good at developing emotional advertisements, or building emotion into your website, or incorporating emotional and bonding moments into a stump speech (a speech delivered repeatedly), perhaps others on your campaign team may be able to assist you and judge accordingly.

CHAPTER 4
DEFINING "SELF"

4.1 BRAND

POSITIVE PERSONAL BRANDING IS THE ART OF becoming known, respected, liked and trusted. All four of these aspects matter when it comes to a candidate becoming elected or electable. A brand is based on a history and is a set of expectations or memories that collectively account for what others determine to be who you are. Many aspects in this chapter are about communicating and shaping that brand so that those who do not know you see that brand as someone they can relate to and eventually vote for.

Branding demands commitment to its portrayal or to its re-invention. It can be said that "a brand is a brand is a brand." In other words, your brand is what others know and see it to be and is not easily changed or re-imagined just because you wish it to be.

When it comes to electability, personal branding involves managing your name and in particular your last name. It is important to communicate your name as part of your brand because it is the only thing that you initially have to offer to a stranger – the stranger who is looking to vote for someone.

An example of the importance of your last name is that your last name will likely be listed preceding your first name on a ballot. The last name may trigger an image for some people, whether or not they have met you or know you. The image may be based on your nationality, your ethnicity, your gender, your religion or even race. To some voters none of those things matter and to others it does. But each of those and more are part of your brand. You cannot change your last name (quickly); it is who you are, and you must capitalize on that last name to further nurture the brand. As an example, when delivering a speech, begin the speech stating your name and at the end of the speech repeat your last name perhaps even once or twice. While it is you and your brand they are voting for, it is equally important for you to remember that it is your last name people are putting the checkmark beside when alone in the voting booth.

Why does this matter? It matters because you wish for people to remember your last name, the centrepiece of your brand for voting purposes. If the last name that you normally use is different than what is required to legally be on the ballot, this will need to become clear in your campaign. It will no doubt need to be your legal last name that is officially on the ballot. If you are considering running for elected office, check all your email accounts, social media accounts etc., to ensure your last name is clear to assist the voter in remembering it.

The brand of a party will often trump the brand that you have as an individual. The brand of your party leader may also trump any personal branding work that you do as an individual. Blending your personal brand with your party brand, either provincially, territorially or federally will be critically important for your election success in partisan voting.

In partisan politics, voters may overlook the name of the candidate (you) and vote for the party or a party leader. As such, "hitching your wagon" to the leadership pony or the party pony may or may not be an advantage, but it may be required because you may not have been given a choice by the party or the leader to do otherwise.

A good example of brand consistency across Canada (30-year longevity) is the Green Party. Most Canadians understand the brand, the colouring, the name, the longevity and the broad philosophy of what it stands for. The Green Party has a brand beginning with its name.

Other elements of your brand that you may or may not wish to use are your education credentials. Advanced education, degrees, designations, post-secondary education, trades certification, etc. are all important to highlight.

It is absolutely encouraged and expected that any degrees, letters or designations that belong after your name are used in any materials that you publish. While there may be some who would not vote for someone because of their added credentials (or their MBA designation as an example), on balance such additional education attained demonstrates a past willingness and ability to learn, invest and even sacrifice.

Anyone who might be wear a uniform for their career is wise to include any related designation and associated photography. Police, military, nurses and firefighters, are examples that must be used to demonstrate part of the history or brand that describes you.

If part of your history and brand includes significant coaching or other youth-related activities, that forms part of your history and brand as well and should be considered and is strongly encouraged to be included in communication materials. Time spent as a teacher, coach, guide, scout leader or teacher's aide are all elements of a brand demonstrating an interest in youth.

While there are many elements of branding, demonstrating to the voting public your history is critical as it is who you are and who you were. Whether it be a leader, a volunteer, an educator, or a professional career person, the public needs and deserves to know more about you. While you may not have many of these career or life experiences, and perhaps you are seeking office at the age of 18, demonstrating to others your history (and your brand) is still critical for you to share with the public for them to be informed voters.

Once I attended a provincial party candidate nomination forum where there were seven candidates (none of whom I knew whatsoever) seeking nomination for a provincial riding. I did not have a vote and went to the meeting with the intent of learning and observing. I actually attended during the time that I was running for a councillor; I thought that I could learn something by observing, because all the candidates there were strangers to me. What I gleaned most was their branding, as I did not care about their actual platforms.

When speaking and in their campaign materials, they each communicated their brand differently.

> Candidate 1 campaigned that night on her family values.
> Candidate 2 campaigned on what she learned in school and how that carried her forward in life.
> Candidate 3 ran on fiscal restraint in everything he spoke of.
> Candidate 4 ran on five issues and was clear on each of the five.
> Candidate 5 ran on his reputation as he openly self-described himself as "a good ole boy" in the area.
> Candidate 6 ran on a list that was so long it was difficult to synthesize.
> Candidate 7 rambled incoherently, and I could not ascertain much about him, similar to Candidate 6.

Interestingly, the "good ole boy" won the nomination. He was so well known that his name was synonymous with the community, I learned later. He had name recognition, and it overshadowed anything else in that contest. We need to become clear on what we can share with people about who we are, what we stand for and about our past, and we need to be able to do that in as few words as possible, in writing and when speaking. This is not always an easy task.

Finally, people want to know your story. As a leader, you will need to recount your story, your history. Is your story one of originality, one of hardship or one of rebirth? Is it one of a voyage, a quest or a hybrid of these? If your audience connects to the story that you articulate, you will become more significant emotionally to them and relatable to them, thus laying a critical foundation for your brand.

For the candidate at that forum, the brand as a "good ole boy," along with his name resonated that night with 100 people in a highly rural area on the prairies who were mostly over the age of 65 years old. He knew how to communicate his brand.

"Hello, my name is Bob Jones, and I am a good ole boy; vote Jones, Bob Jones."

4.2 IMAGE

Today we have many stereotypes and particularly many biases when we imagine others based on little knowledge and information. Because of this, the image that you portray with your photography, dress code, appearance etc. requires thoughtfulness. To those who know you well, who work with you, and play with you or otherwise do not need to do much research on you, much of the image information does not matter at all. To most voters, however, it does matter. Most voters do not know you.

It is important that you be authentic; if you are working to re-invent yourself during an election campaign, that may only work for a limited number of people. You must first maintain your authenticity. Your closest colleagues and family members will question your integrity if there is a substantial change to your image during an election. Faking an accent, for example, would be unwise (and it has been attempted).

All that said, personal branding can be improved upon during a short-term election period. Dress code, conduct and personal hygiene are all examples of areas that can cause upside and downside interpretation of you by those who would normally be strangers or to those who come to learn about you on social media, etc. On that account, those areas where you maintain authenticity for those who know you and solidify an image for those who do not know you (or who have never seen you), are important to consider.

It would be terribly unwise for me to describe to you what changes you should make to your image to portray a brand, because that is a personal preference. However, you need to be thoughtful about all those matters that influence the opportunity to make a good first impression. After all, you only get one opportunity to provide a good first impression.

We all observe others in normal day-to-day life outside of an election campaign who work to change an image or appearance. Losing weight, dying hair or changing an entire dress code are examples of such changes. The closer this makeover occurs to an election campaign, the less authentic it may seem to some. To others who have never seen you, it may be important for your image and brand.

Thus, the image you wish to portray to those who know you and to those who have never met you, seen you or heard you is extremely personal and wise to establish early on.

4.3 COLOURS

I once read somewhere, "I have never seen the colours of black and white or black and yellow be successful for election campaign colours." I do not know if this is true or not, but it was one of my considerations when I chose colours for my election materials the first time.

The colours you choose and the rest of brand design can go hand in hand. Research colours and what they mean to the voting public. This changes over time and should be considered, as a candidate needs to think through the colours that best portray their brand and image.

I have seen rainbow colours for intentional imaging and branding. I have seen pink used for intentional imaging and branding. Some will use the official colours adopted by their community. The colours of your party affiliation is another important consideration.

It is critical to use two colours that are contrasting, because it is the last name that must pop out in materials and online. If you use black on white (which I do not recommend), design your materials so that your last name pops out. When you design buttons, badges, brochures, a letterhead, websites and lawn signs, stick with the same colour scheme for an entire campaign.

Colours can also assist in the vibrancy of images. Yellow, for example, is a vibrant and uplifting colour and it is easy for a darker colour to be used in contrast with yellow. Your last name needs to pop out, and a darker blue or black can easily pop out on yellow.

You will notice that the chosen party colours in Canada in the territories and in the provinces are usually colour coded, logo coded and branded quite consistently across an entire jurisdiction. This approach has distinct advantages and may even be the reason for election success. If the branding, imagery and colouring are distinct, widespread and recognizable, it can create the image of a wave of support. Seeing a lot of red or a lot of green or a lot of blue or a lot of orange at every street corner, on hundreds of lawns, at roadsides or on fences can create for that particular party the image of domination and governing power.

Any candidate at any order can learn from the branding of partisan political parties in Canada. These Canadian parties have developed such imagery and colours through research and design work that is intentional and appealing.

When designing signs, brochures and other materials that are seen by the voters should be coloured on both sides. For example, if you use yellow as a base colour, ensure that both sides of the signage or the brochure cardstock are yellow.

4.4 PHOTOGRAPHY

Photography and imagery become synonymous with the brand. It is no surprise that elected officials and candidates work to obtain photos (staged or not) taken together with a variety of demographics, socioeconomic groups and more.

Emotional connection matter. Whether the imagery and photography include photos with family, parents, children, the elderly, the homeless, the wealthy, the superheroes, the famous, athletes, friends or animals – in other countries, at romantic places, at sunrise or sunset, it works.

Voters look for reasons to connect with someone and there are many aspects to that. Of course, people you know or who are related to you is one way of attracting votes. People who like the things that you like is another reason those people may vote for you. People who have similar beliefs are yet another reason. Of course, some voters cast their ballot for those who are different because of their belief in seeking diversity. But a picture or series of pictures of someone are snapshots of what that person may see as important. A picture of a candidate horseback riding, a picture in a farmyard or with farm animals will surely conjure up different emotions or beliefs about a person than about someone whose only photos are in high-rise towers, on subways or at cocktail parties. While the imagery may not represent who the person actually is, given our experiences and belief patterns established over the years, we may choose to vote based on some of that imagery. Emotions matter, and those images that tug at emotions are much more effective than head shots or stock photos. Demonstrating that you can be comfortable being with both "queens and paupers" is equally important.

Additionally, imagery from where you reside matters. If you are running in the province of Saskatchewan, it is wise to have Saskatchewan photos. Similarly, if you are on the coastal waters, having a picture of the beach or ocean is important to your brand, your voters and election success. While photo locations may seem to be common sense, it is always surprising to see how so many candidates do not take the location of their photography seriously for their campaign materials. Just as in written material and online imagery, since it is part of your brand and history, any photography that depicts you in uniform for some of your career is wise to be included within your campaign imagery. As shared earlier, police, military, nurses and firefighters are good examples of elements that help to describes you.

Ensure that you have ONE personal photo that you use as your "go-to" photo for consistency purposes. That photo should be non-controversial, simple and the image that you want everyone to relate to. You will have other photos, but this one photo is your "go-to" photo.

4.5 LOGO

At the party level, most candidates honour and adopt the logo of their party. This is wise as that is the connection that the voters hope to make with the candidate, and vice versa. If you are not running under a party banner and are running as an independent or as a locally elected official, the logo will need to be more personal.

There are a few logo tips that should be kept in mind. First of all, do not rob one off the internet that seems trendy or attractive. If you are caught doing so, there may be legal implications, and it is plain wrong. You may pay the political price if caught.

Additionally, it is not permitted that you use the logo of the parent organization that you are seeking an office in. If you are running for a town councillor, the logo of that town is for the use of that town itself or that entity and is not public property to be borrowed and used by a candidate running for office.

If you are considering a logo, there are two additional important elements to consider. First, keep it simple. Few are going to attempt to interpret your logo; therefore, anything complicated does not add value. Secondly, build your last name into your logo so that it is visible and legible. The importance of your last name cannot be underestimated, and if you are able to incorporate it into a simple logo, that can be even better.

Additionally, letterhead and logo and name should all be branded and commensurate with each other. An image of attention to detail creates a subliminal message that the candidate is thoughtful and pays attention to the little things.

Figure 5. *Letterhead*

Finally, colouring and fit matter. The logo, letterhead, signage, brochures, website, blogs and more must all be consistent so that the voting public does not have to "go looking" to understand who the candidate is. We need to remember that it is possible that there are more people who vote for you who do not know you than those who do know you.

4.6 SLOGAN OR TAGLINE

Again, like the logos and colours, at the party level, candidates should honour and adopt any party slogan. This is wise, as the connections that the voters make with the candidate are often to the party or to the leader of that party and not to an individual candidate. If you are not running as part of a party and are running as an independent or for a local office, the slogan would be personal.

If you choose to use a slogan, keep in mind that no one can get inside your head to understand any deep meaning you might intend; therefore, you will need to keep it generic, and make sure there is no controversy attached to it. Researching logos in other jurisdictions and online is clearly acceptable but using a registered corporate logo may be problematic. While slogans are simply a collection of words that you can feel free to duplicate from other parts of the country, logos are much more sensitive. Including your name in a logo helps set it apart from others so that no one will claim that it from being a registered logo.

If you adopt a slogan, use it on letterhead, stationery, websites, business cards, blogs and more. Maintain any colour theme that you have adopted as well as combine it with your logo. Putting together an entire brand and image allows others to see you as complete.

You may also wish to include your slogan and your logo with your photo all times. Be seen as a complete candidate.

4.7 ONLINE IMAGE AND PRESENCE

Generally speaking, your online presence should be thought out well in advance of you running. While it is not always possible, it is advisable to clean any online presence that is no longer what you wish your image and brand to be. Facebook, Twitter, YouTube, Instagram, dating sites or any other social media posting should be scoured by you for content that you would no longer like to be associated with. While your footprint may not always be able to be completely altered or changed or deleted, there is much one can do to minimize damage caused by any postings that may no longer fit with one's views. People change, people evolve, and something that might have been posted or which happened 15 years ago may no longer be an opinion today. Unfortunately, the voting public or those who wish to "go low," will use that information to harm your chances. Dates of a post may even get removed, altered or manipulated by others to harm your image and electability.

The flip side is also true. I am aware of someone who was a senior member of a Liberal party who told a potential candidate that their Facebook posts were not Liberal enough and that they needed to add Liberal-leaning content quickly or they would not be seen as favourable by the voters who would be scouring their conservative-leaning Facebook posts.

Our email history is another story. Someone who archives a lot of emails from the past may find reasons to raise something that was in an email months and years ago that may be harmful or helpful to your campaign depending on the situation. We have less control over our email history.

Finally, the results that emerge when searching a person's name using Google cannot be altered because of Google's policies, and how Google records traffic will leave a footprint that cannot be easily altered without expensive and time-consuming legal intervention with the Google Company. Therefore, if there is anything that is untoward as part of your searchable Google history, you will need to be willing and prepared to address the questions raised throughout a campaign. Opposing candidates or campaigns may choose to use your Google history to "go low." Similarly, if you are working on a campaign that has decided to "go low," you will need to ensure your own history is clean. "Those who live in glass houses should not throw stones." If your Google history contains great content and is long, it is an advantage.

4.8 SOCIAL MEDIA, BLOGGING AND THE WEBSITE

In today's political environment, and indeed in this day and age, several avenues of communication are required to reach a variety of audiences. The need for a social media presence today is likely required for someone to become elected.

The public receives information from their elected officials in a variety of ways, and the old-fashioned letters are becoming less and less frequent as a tool used to ask and answer questions. Clearly, during an election campaign, significant letter writing will be nearly nonexistent. Anyone contemplating running for office needs to consider having Facebook, LinkedIn, Twitter and Instagram accounts at minimum. More and more candidates are also creating a YouTube channel, and having all these avenues in place is fundamentally important. The sooner these platforms are in place, the sooner that information can be disseminated and distributed using these approaches, and the more followers and links you will have far in advance of any election campaign. The easier it is to communicate messages during an election campaign, the better. These platforms will continue to be necessary for communicating with others as an elected official if you are successful at the ballot box. For example, I have approximately 4,000 Twitter followers, approximately 1,000 LinkedIn connections and approximately 5,000 Facebook friends. That makes a difference to being able to communicate my message and brand.

Some elected officials or candidates attempt to separate their public candidate accounts from accounts that are personal and private, but indeed, it is nearly impossible and I would discourage it. You will not be able to convince anyone that they need to search in order to determine when you are a regular citizen not seeking election, when you are an elected official or when you are seeking to become elected. I have seen many attempts by individuals to keep their accounts and communications separate. It is usually a failure and an exercise in futility. Your brand is your brand.

It is, however, possible that the official office of an elected body or role has its own Twitter account, as an example, and when the office holds the account, it is then the responsibility of the user of that account to treat it as a public account. It is owned and operated as a publicly funded and publicly owned account. The "Office of the Prime Minister," the "Office of the Premier," the "Office of the Mayor," the "Office of the Chief" and the "Office of the Reeve" are examples of publicly owned and operated accounts. Even use of these accounts become blurry when postings and their uses are not clearly established. Candidates and elected officials need to ensure that the uses are clearly established and delineated. An account of the "Office of the Mayor," as an example, goes from one mayor to another mayor to the next mayor in theory.

During election campaigning, the use of all the candidate and personal accounts are important ways to communicate your brand, your message, your photos, your videos, your brochures, your last name and more. You are able to use these approaches to reach many audiences that speaking, phoning and letter writing cannot.

As mentioned previously (and it is worth repeating), if you have accounts that do not clearly articulate or use your last name that will actually show on the ballot, you should update these accounts. Some people, when they create their personal accounts, may swap their first and last names to be coy, may use nicknames or use social media handles that have no relevance to the individual's brand or name; some use only their first and second name on their accounts. Becoming standard and ensuring your last name is within these accounts is important so that the candidate is properly known to the voter, as well as to ensure that it does not come across that you are hiding something from others. Email addresses are much more difficult for some people to change quickly because of the history that most individuals have with their email accounts, but it too should be considered. With the ability to have email addresses automatically forwarded to another email address available, this should be a consideration. For example, an email address such as uglydayoutside2022@hotmail.com will not be the best email address to use when one is running as an election candidate compared to an email address with your last name included in it.

Additionally, candidates should have a website, and if you have the resources or someone on your campaign team who can help drive traffic to and populate your website regularly with information, you are wise to use that person's skills if you cannot do it yourself. Adding photos, branding information, voting stations, contact information, donor information, volunteer information, blogs and more assists in the name recognition and ultimately assists in a successful campaign. This history also assists an incumbent in adding to the information and building a collection of data that may assist in future campaigns.

It is wise to ensure that your website has a function that allows it to be translated into any number of languages. Additionally, linking together any blogging, LinkedIn, website, Instagram, TikTok, Facebook and Twitter accounts are often done today, and that approach to messaging helps ensure improved consistency, maximum communication and constancy of purpose in branding.

Finally, the use of these media platforms to advertise is common today. Facebook advertising is common and utilizes Facebook and Google data to drive users, followers, donors and voters to your page. While we may feel Google is watching too much of what we are doing, the facts are that using these platforms are a necessary approach for a candidate to promote their candidacy and appeal to voters who are looking to learn and be influenced who to vote for. We take the good with the bad of these traffic drivers. Additionally, there are website experts who are able to assist the candidate in ensuring that their name, social media posts, and website rises closer to the top of Google's first page. There are techniques and costs to do this that should be explored. If you can afford to do so, I would encourage you to employ someone or at least find volunteers who are willing and able to assist you in this technical aspect of campaigning, if you do not have the required skills to do so yourself.

4.9 WHAT NOT TO DO

Post nothing that the typical voting public would see as inappropriate. Most of us know what crosses the line.

Illegal or unethical approaches have a digital footprint, and those candidates who have a history of such conduct will usually be exposed at almost all levels of governing. Avoid contact and engagement with any such activity within your circle of relationships. All activities, good and bad, form part of your brand.

Do not confuse the voter with names (nicknames), different first and last names or other confusing techniques. Do not use an email address or social media account name that is likely offensive to anyone. Again, most of us know what is and what is not an offensive name or email address, regardless of what your intentions are.

Never post, email or communicate any offensive material, and if there are any such offensive materials contained within any of your sites, you should remove such materials. Of course, retweeting and marking as favourites can be equally problematic. The list of inappropriateness is long, yet most know what is inappropriate and what is not.

CHAPTER 5

BUDGET, SPENDING AND FUNDRAISING

5.1 WHY PEOPLE GIVE

THERE ARE A VARIETY OF REASONS WHY people donate to election campaigns. One can never predict the reasons why people do or don't donate, who may donate, the amounts that individuals or companies are willing to donate, their motives and other details that are not required to be disclosed.

Reasons for donating include for tax purposes, supporting a candidate, supporting a cause, supporting a party, for philanthropy purposes and to demonstrate support for democracy. Some donate believing there is a quid pro quo inferred. In these instances, the candidate should avoid honouring any such inference stated or otherwise. Also, some companies or leaders wish to be known as highly political, while others hold openly stated values to remain apolitical for other reasons. Corporate donation strategies are consistent with the culture that is known within that organization. Some companies and individuals wish to show their support for a party or individual to become a more well-known company, and others wish for their support to be extremely private and personal.

There are some jurisdictions where campaigns are permitted to be self-funded, and the disclosure rules are such that the details associated with this may vary from jurisdiction to jurisdiction or may vary from one order of government to another order. Candidates who wish to self-fund often do so to ensure they are not beholden to anyone and in particular to avoid any inferred favour, real or perceived. Some candidates have low-cost campaigns, while others simply cannot raise adequate funds to make a big difference.

One may never know why people or company decision-makers give or encourage giving. Some companies have written policies explicitly stating their political donor or support approach.

It is also common for all members of the same family to each donate to the same candidate or one party for various reasons.

5.2 WHO TO ASK

Just like we do not know the connections that many have to others when it comes to any support or voting (six degrees of separation), the same holds true for those who are willing and able to donate. It is clear that we do not know the financial capacity of individuals or corporations and the ability and willingness to donate cannot be easily judged. Donations may flow from those who appear to have the least ability to give, yet some individuals known to be wealthiest are not prepared to permit any of their resources to go to any party or candidate in any fashion. Publicly traded companies in particular have significant considerations in this regard, because shareholders are a wide variety of individuals.

There is an adage, "The 'no' you already have, the 'yes' you have to ask for," and it rings true when it comes to asking for donations. When asking for funds, it is best to err on the side of simply asking because you simply never know.

Friends and family should be given the opportunity to support someone, although asking relatives, neighbours and friends can also pose its own challenges. Asking those the closest to you may be best handled by you or perhaps a third party with a high degree of discretion, tact and confidentiality. Since it is common for donations to come from more than one member of the same family (such as both spouses donating to provincial candidates), it is simply OK to ask a family to discuss the idea of a donation.

Asking for an amount is most likely inappropriate and sharing with others to donate "what you think you can afford or are prepared to donate" is usually the best strategy.

I have received funds from complete strangers, high school classmates, friends and companies. Similarly, I did not receive any funds from some who I thought might be prepared to donate. One just does not know where the support may or may not come from.

5.3 WHO ASKS

While it may be wise for a third party to do the asking for funds, it may be the desire of the donor to donate directly to the candidate at a face-to-face meeting, breakfast or lunch. While time may be short for someone on a campaign trail, if someone is known to be a financial contributor, time must be found to connect with that individual. It may even be awkward since donors may be friends or strangers and the money can be understood to be a personal commitment. It can be humbling, yet being grateful to someone for providing cash or gifts in kind is the nature of election campaigns in Canada. Therefore, we must not be surprised by this approach and we must never be surprised by anything that may arise when it comes to fundraising.

Again, since in most cases a third party is required for reporting and financial tracking of funds, if a candidate can find the right person to also be the person to seek funds, that is a bonus. Someone who can do banking, do accounting, do bookkeeping and ask for donations, is a valuable member of any campaign team and will tend to keep the candidate out of financial challenges and awkward spots. A third party also allows families and friends to be much more open about their reasons for a decision or amounts being donated.

5.4 BUDGET

Like in so many financial aspects of our lives, a campaign budget is critical and necessary to ensure that everyone involved in the financial side of the campaign understands what can and what cannot be done. To have someone spending a lot of money on signage and advertising and not having any regard for the budget is a formula for disaster. There are many stories of candidates and campaigns needing to collect money long after an election, not being able to pay bills and having to spend a lot of personal money based on decisions that were out of the candidate's hands.

As a candidate, you are the captain of your own ship and therefore need to ensure the financial side is well managed. Budget planning, spending adherence and ensuring the amount being spent does not exceed the funds being raised, in the end lays in the lap of the candidate and no one else.

Additionally, the public will likely sooner or later be made aware when a candidate was not able to meet their financial obligations. Therefore, a budget is critical to ensuring some degree of adherence is maintained. Like many spreadsheets in this process, keeping things simple with an Excel spreadsheet allows others to access and view line-by-line costs and revenues. Excel can be opened on most smart phones and computers and is easily understood without much explanation.

The KISS principle applies to budget, revenue and expenditures (Keep It Simple Stupid).

This figure is an example of a budget that may trigger some ideas as to how you put your expenses spreadsheet together.

Figure 6. *Budget and expenditures*

Budget Item	Budget Amount	Actual to date	Projected total	Needed $
Banking	$100	$75	$167	$92
Office	$1,500	$845	$845	$0
Food for Office	$500	$0	$75	$75
Office Supplies	$1,000	$57	$97	$40
Office Utilities	$600	$0	$150	$150
Office Signage	$250	$0	$410	$410
Gifts	$1,000	$10	$260	$250
Website	$2,000	$0	$2,000	$2,000
Photography	$150	$260	$260	$0
Business Cards	$350	$302	$302	$0
Lawn and street signs	$1,500	$1,592	$1,592	$0
Sign Stakes	$1,250	$835	$875	$40
Stationery	$200	$568	$718	$150
Large 4 x 8 Signs	$1,000	$2,181	$2,181	$0
Postage for general	$1,250	$787	$1,037	$250
Canada Post mailout	$1,000	$0	$250	$250
Newspaper Ads	$5,000	$1,077	$4,589	$3,512
Printer Cartridges	$500	$638	$913	$275
Maps	$25	$0	$35	$35
20,000 door knocking cards	$1,500	$988	$988	$0
Billboard	$3,000	$3,350	$3,350	$0
Brochure	$1,500	$0	$2,067	$2,067
Kickoff	$1,000	$0	$2,050	$2,050
Election day	$2,000	$0	$950	$950
Gas	$0	$352	$417	$65
Contingency	$1,409	$696	$1,329	$633
Totals	$29,584	$14,613	$27,907	$13,294

Projected total	$27,907
In Account	$14,613
Fundraising needed	$13,294

5.5 KEEPING A DATABASE

The spreadsheet in Chapter 2 is an example of the database to keep for donors.

Keep track of all donors, all amounts, mailing addresses plus a paper copy or electronic trail of all donations and expenditures so that financial disclosure can be completed accurately at some time. Today, with a significant number of online transfers occurring, at times it may be difficult to track or recall what amounts were paid to whom or donated from whom based on limited, or even cryptic, banking information alone. Attention to detail in this regard by the financial oversight person or persons is critical to be able to meet all disclosure requirements at the end of an election cycle.

Additionally, a list of donors, mailing addresses and other contact information allows for proper thanking of donors, submission of receipts, etc. at the conclusion of the election campaign.

The same principle applies to gifts in kind as to cash donations. Keep the data, place a fair market value on the donation and ensure it is properly recorded for recording accuracy, legal requirements and meeting the needs of a donor.

5.6 FUNDRAISING IDEAS AND TACTICS

When it comes to raising funds for a campaign, the approach will certainly depend on the amount needed, the order of government being sought and the degree of partisanship that the campaign entails. There are some key principles to follow for all fundraising efforts.

First, the best approach is to ask or have someone ask on your behalf. While asking is not a novel idea, it is the most effective tactic that one can employ.

Second, having a campaign team or finance manager who is unafraid to ask is an important element of fundraising success.

Third, make the giving easy. Consider mailing a self-addressed stamped envelope to someone who is willing (or is believed to be willing) to donate, with a personal message from the candidate contained within.

A fourth principle is that goods or gifts in kind are often easier to obtain than cash. A business or individual may be willing to donate office space, thank-you cards, stationery, business cards or lawn sign stakes. In that way, the donor knows where the money is going, may be able to claim the donation if tax laws permit it, and the product or service is something they have available and can donate with ease. I recall a lumber company having a surplus of wooden stakes that they were pleased to get rid of and the campaign team was willing to take as it helped cleanup the lumber yard for the donor. Again, following all the reporting and recording laws matter for proper reporting.

The larger and more diverse a campaign team is, the higher the probability of obtaining donations. Just like any aspect of a campaign, it is always surprising who knows who when it comes to possible donors. Human connections to obtain donations are multiplied when a candidate has a strong and diverse team.

While there are legal requirements for using crowdfunding platforms such as GoFundMe, there are numerous online approaches as simple as a Facebook post, a Twitter post or a link on one's website to make an appeal or make donating easier.

A good fundraiser event may bring together a team representing a cross section of the community or constituency. Motivating people is an important job for a good fundraising chair, and ideas such as a donor gathering, a barbeque or a party are all examples of how funds can be raised. Fundraising is not a job for the timid, and a feature of a good fundraising campaign is to keep the activists updated as to where the fundraising stands. This is especially important for political parties and less important for councillors or school board officials.

One rule of thumb for fundraising is to attempt to ask in such a way that "no" is not an easy answer. You should not ask for an amount, and if you do choose to specify an amount, never ask for too little, and you may even choose to ask more than once. The list of potential contributors often includes friends, neighbours, relatives, acquaintances and anyone else you know. Strangers are the most difficult to obtain funds or gifts in kind from, unless the strangers are donating to a party. That said, picking the techniques or approaches that you are comfortable with from those listed in this chapter will assist you in maximizing your fundraising results.

5.7 BANKING

Create a bank account if there is any cash that needs to change hands in a campaign. Most campaigns are not self-funded, therefore the need for a third party to administer and hold funds is a necessary consideration for everyone involved. A bank account does not eliminate the potential for theft or fraud, but it clearly adds a level of professionalism, thoroughness and objectivity to any campaign. A cash-only campaign is fraught with potential difficulties and holds suspicion for all involved.

All banking transactions should have two signatures, or if only one signature is planned, the signature should not be that of the candidate. Again, a third-party approach reduces suspicion and any nefarious activity that may occur.

At the end of the campaign, ensure that the bank account information is communicated to the authorities and if a campaign is legally permitted to carry the bank account and amounts forward for a future election, this information needs to be adequately managed and reported. Closing of accounts also carries obligations in most jurisdictions, as the campaign team and the financial oversight personnel must ensure that the legal and ethical approaches are taken in this regard.

Some orders and some jurisdictions permit political action committees, and if one is formed and used, there must be research into its formation, use and reporting. When I was finally finished my last term in office, I had nearly $10,000 remaining in the election account; the account was closed and all funds donated to a children's mental health association, a good example of what may be done with remaining funds. Copies of all transactions were provided to the election returning officer.

5.8 THE MYTHS

There are many myths when it comes to fundraising, campaigning and general financial matters within campaigns.

First, it is a myth that all campaigns need a lot of funds to ensure someone becomes elected. While there is often some correlation between spending and the number of votes received, there are also many examples of great door knocking campaigns, and addressing the details noted in the previous chapters can be done very inexpensively. I recall one campaign where a candidate had a pre-recorded robocall go to 20,000 home phone numbers (before cell phones were popular), costing a substantial amount of money. This candidate spent the most money of any candidate on that election campaign and finished nearly last in a field of 21 candidates vying for six spots. I am also aware of a university student who mobilized a substantial team of people of all ages and spent very little money. He finished near the top of votes attained by all the candidates in a large election.

It is a myth that rich people donate to campaigns. As said earlier, one must not judge who may donate.

Candidates come from all walks of life, and it is a myth to believe that because someone enters a contest, they have funds to begin with. Some may and some may not, and therefore, any number of truisms may exist when it comes to elected officials. I recall a grade six student one time asked me, "Do you live in a mansion?" Equating fame and personal wealth is a misjudgment that is not uncommon. Most candidates enter a contest knowing that raising funds will be required, and most members of the public generally understand that campaign fundraising in Canada is common. What the public needs to know is that the money donated is generally well managed. It is a myth that money is poorly managed by candidates; funds are generally well managed.

It is a myth that because someone has been convicted, guilty or rumoured of a wrongdoing that the public will automatically reject that person at the ballot box. Equally, donors may be willing to support that person. There are examples in Canadian history where those who have served jail time or have been removed from office or found guilty of a crime are elected or re-elected by their constituents. Anyone can mount a successful campaign with the right team plus a team with the ability to raise funds.

Finally, donors (and voters) are forgiving, have short memories and are willing to assist a candidate who is known to them or perhaps was nominated within the ideology they subscribe to. The willingness of Canadians to forgive and forget is always a remarkable trait that we should be proud of. While one's past may lead to difficult financial situations during and after an election campaign, I repeat what I said earlier in this chapter that we can never predict the reasons or predict who may wish to donate to whom or the amounts they are willing to donate.

5.9 ONLINE

Online banking is very common for transferring of funds and makes donating easy. Ease of donating makes a big difference for donors. Most of us have experienced challenges with filling in online forms or navigating from one step to another when going through an online donation process. If you make this approach easy and secure and are able to communicate it to many people, this approach ensures an electronic trail exists. It also ensures that names of donors are available for follow-up to be completed. It also may permit the maximum amounts to be raised.

For these reasons, make the social media or website links easy to use, and secure. Many new tools exist for donating, and most Canadians will assess whether a site or approach is secure.

5.10 CONSISTENCY WITH THE LAWS

A variety of laws, acts, local policies or required procedures exist relative to the limits, corporate donations, disclosure and formats that are necessary to be adhered to. Candidates or those wishing to be candidates must familiarize themselves with these requirements on all aspects, and this is particularly important for financial aspects of a campaign.

Some donors wish to remain anonymous, and if the laws of the jurisdiction permit this, it should be respected by the campaign. Some jurisdictions permit cash donations, while others require all donations to be accounted for donor by donor.

As stated earlier, there are some jurisdictions where campaigns are permitted to be self-funded and the disclosure rules vary, so the details associated with this may vary from jurisdiction to jurisdiction.

The requirement for a financial agent or some form of independent financing oversight may or may not be spelled out in the legislation, but it is wise to use a third-party agent.

Figure 7. *Example of one financial disclosure form*

Vote ☒ Elections Calgary

Form #5 (EC-05-01-CA-05)

Candidate Financial Information
Local Authorities Election Act (Section 27)

Local Jurisdiction: The City of Calgary, Province of Alberta

The personal information on this form is being collected to support the administrative requirements of local authorities election process and is authorized under sections 21 and 27 of the Local Authorities Election Act and section 33(c) of the Freedom of Information and Protection of Privacy Act. The personal information will be managed in compliance with the privacy provisions of the Freedom of Information and Protection of Privacy Act. If you have any questions concerning the collection of this personal information, please contact the Deputy City Clerk, Elections at (403) 476-4100 or candidates@calgary.ca.

Candidate's Information

Name ______________________

Address ______________________ Postal Code ____________

Address of place(s) where candidate records are maintained

1. Address ______________________ Postal Code ____________
2. Address ______________________ Postal Code ____________
3. Address ______________________ Postal Code ____________

Name(s), address(es), and signing authorities of financial institutions where campaign contributions will be deposited

1. Financial Institution ______________________
   Address ______________________ Postal Code ____________
   Signing Authority ______________________
2. Financial Institution ______________________
   Address ______________________ Postal Code ____________
   Signing Authority ______________________
3. Financial Institution ______________________
   Address ______________________ Postal Code ____________
   Signing Authority ______________________

Where there is any change in the above-mentioned information, the candidate shall notify the local jurisdiction in writing within 48 hours of such changes by submitting a completed information form.

ISC: Unrestricted   Page 1 of 1

5.11 DIRECT MAIL SUCCESS

While perhaps successful with some elections, usually mail-out donation requests are not highly successful for donor adherence. This is especially true in the modern times of online banking and e-Transfers. Mail-outs no longer yield the results that they once did. While the pandemic of 2020–2021 had an effect on many matters, one thing it did do was increase the number of individuals in Canada who moved to online banking, and this should be considered when seeking funds.

5.12 THE DIRECT ASK

As stated earlier, the direct ask is the best approach to fundraising for an election campaign. It is equally important that there is a coordinated effort for these direct asks. It is critical for the campaign team member who is responsible for the ask, also tracks who is asking and who is being asked so that two separate campaign workers do not ask the same donor. While errors may be made in a fast-moving campaign period, it is important that tracking mechanisms are in place for errors to be avoided.

5.13 WHAT NOT TO DO

Do not take any shortcuts when it comes to disclosure or tracking.

Do not brag about, complain about or disclose any information about donors or money-related matters (other than making disclosures that are required by law). "Loose lips sink ships," and that is truer when it comes to money than perhaps in any other area of campaigning.

Do not break any law, act or policy, federally or in any jurisdiction requiring full disclosure and adherence to the law.

Do not ignore paying any bill.

Do not forget to thank donors in special ways.

Do not make any false financial claims whatsoever on the revenue or expenditure side.

Do not rely solely on yourself as a candidate to get it all 100% correct. Ask for a third party to review and/or lead financial matters to ensure adherence. This is worth the time and resources to do.

Do not forget to close out bank accounts when you are done serving as an elected official if the accounts were dedicated to your campaign. If funds were able to be legally rolled over to a political party or donated to another future candidate, make that happen. If a balance had to be donated or otherwise dispersed, do not forget to do this.

Do not underestimate the scrutiny that the public will have on money. Donations to candidates is viewed by many as public money and is transparently displayed. There will be self-proclaimed auditors of your financials.

CHAPTER 6
THE CAMPAIGN PLAN AND TACTICS

6.1 THE 7 P'S OF PLANNING

IT IS SAID THAT PROPER PRIOR PLANNING Prevents Pathetically Poor Performance. This is certainly true for planning an election campaign, which requires the utmost care and attention to detail.

Election and campaign planning span many aspects from data collection to marketing to leading a team to image management and many more in between. Of course, there are examples periodically where someone is elected "accidentally" when their name is included on a ballot for the purposes of rounding out a slate or ensuring someone is representing each riding in a provincial, territorial or federal election. Those instances are rare. In some elections when someone puts their name forward and is acclaimed, minimal planning is required, and therefore the details are less important. If you enter or assist a race against a competitor with the objective to win, the tactics used only achieve the election goal if you have a thoughtful plan that permits success for the candidate and for those assisting the candidate.

Attention to detail matters, and this chapter covers that process.

6.2 THE TACTICS

Contained within this book are a multitude of to-dos that require thought and perhaps a plan to execute. Each of these to-dos requires an assessment by the candidate, the campaign manager and perhaps the campaign team as to whether or not one needs to act upon the many details necessary. The depth and breadth of each to-do is determined by the order of government and the size of the jurisdiction, to name only a couple of factors. The list is different for someone running for mayor in a large county than it is for someone running for councillor in a small community and is again different for someone running for a school trustee.

Here are some broad categories that fit most elections:

1. Administration
2. Launch
3. Data collection
4. Campaign team
5. Brochures
6. Social media
7. Traditional media
8. Finances
9. Candidate image
10. Signage
11. Press
12. Platform
13. Messaging
14. Gimmicks
15. Door knocking
16. Election day
17. Post-election
18. Forums
19. Campaign headquarters
20. Schedule

Once your organization structure is in place, and your top team members are in place, you can group any number of these under the responsibility of those who are able to lead the effort.

6.3 ASSIGNING RESPONSIBILITIES

Depending on the size of your campaign and depending upon the size of the jurisdiction, assigning responsibilities to the above broad categories may be the responsibility of the candidate or the campaign manager. If you have a team of 5 to 10 on the top tier of the campaign team, you may consider assigning captains from this group to lead various aspects of the campaign. The door knocking team, as an example, may be a team of 50 individuals in a city of 750,000 people, while it may be solely the candidate knocking on doors in a village of 600. The breadth and depth of the campaign is also a function of the number of candidates, the distance of travel within the jurisdiction, the time of year (weather conditions), access to various media, internet coverage and more. Consequently, any checklist will not be a one-size-fits-all checklist and must be tailored to match many factors.

Invariably someone will volunteer for something where they are able to take on more, and if they have the candidate's trust and the ability to do so, individuals like this should be entrusted and encouraged to do more. Similarly, it is common for someone to volunteer for a role but not have the time, ability or leadership skills to do what they volunteered to do. It may even be a situation where a volunteer cannot afford the cost (such as gas to do the driving) that was unanticipated at the time the role was assumed by that volunteer. At times, there will be a need to step in and change the roles or add resources such that the person is successful at a role they are able to perform.

The replacement of, elimination of, or demotion of a campaign worker and must be done if necessary, because it is the candidate's reputation or electability that is at stake, and no one person must be allowed to get in the way of the real reason for the effort and the end goal. Tough decisions are needed, and when you can do these changes privately, with compassion and with caring thoughts, you can continue to get that person's support, even though they may not be able to do the job assigned or the job they volunteered to do. This happened to me on a few occasions, including needing to reduce the role and hours of a paid worker because the individual was "in over their head."

6.4 THE LAUNCH

Candidates may wish to be very private about their plans for weeks or even months leading up to a campaign. This may be an intentional tactical plan to avoid media or costs or personal hardship. It may be due to a degree of uncertainty while a candidate gathers intelligence and does their due diligence. As mentioned previously, the launch may also matter to incumbents differently than it might matter to those entering a contest for the first time. Communications delays may be for employment or family reasons, and someone "scooping the candidate" as an insider may cause harm. Regardless of the circumstances, the decision of a launch date is important and must be left to the discretion of the candidate as to the place, time and style of their preference.

There are also other approaches that some potential candidates take, such as requesting someone to leak the possibility of a campaign. This may be a wise approach for some, as the candidate is potentially able to gauge some level of support or lack thereof at no cost and little accountability. Floating a trial balloon is something for a potential candidate to consider but is not often used.

If a candidate is emailing others and checking with others on information prior to any announcement, each time any communication occurs, the potential for rumours to leak or spread is obvious. When it comes to politics and elected office, the leaking of secrets is common and even expected. In politics, there is hardly ever a secret in a sneak attack when it comes to elections.

In some jurisdictions, the public may easily learn about individuals who have filed papers or who have filed their name so that the candidate may begin to explore and begin to spend or collect funds. These financial obligations vary from order to order of elected government as well as across Canada and within provinces and territories. It is critical that anyone who wishes to launch without all matters in place ensures that there is no violation of policy, regulation or act for the jurisdiction in question. Aside from any political consequences, there may also be significant implications that ranges from fines, to sanctions, to disqualification or severe penalties if the appropriate steps are not followed.

For most jurisdictions, there is a requirement for nomination papers to be signed and submitted by a prospective candidate, and while for some, this may also permit the information to remain private for a time, the submission of papers and signatures (and perhaps a deposit) will send the public a signal of one's intentions. Often these nomination papers are publicly available in most jurisdictions in Canada.

A launch and communication plan are opportunities for various things to occur. First, it allows for the obvious declaration of intent and desire to serve. It is an opportunity in many communities for there to be some press coverage. It is an opportunity to get support, find volunteers and raise funds.

A launch location may also matter. If there are multiple press reporters prepared to attend or cover a launch and the announcement, the location may matter significantly. If one is running for a provincial legislature, announcing in front of the legislative building is a good backdrop. It may be wise to make the announcement in front of city hall, in a wheat field or at any number of strategic locations. If another skating facility is needed in a community and is part of a candidate's platform, an announcement at a current skating facility might be wise. A school trustee may wish to announce near a school, with appropriate photos taken.

It may be wise to announce alone, with significant friends, family or others. The location of the announcement should be somewhere within the voting area that one is seeking votes from; otherwise, unintended messaging may occur.

One only gets one chance to make a first impression, and considerations of dress code and other visuals may matter to those who attend the event. Whether it be photos for posterity, for advertising, for Instagram posts or for what may become a front-page story, how the visual is viewed may matter and needs to be considered. An announcement may also include a campaign team or supporters, and when this occurs, there will be a tendency by viewers to

THE POLITICAL CAMPAIGN "HOW-TO" GUIDE

assess diversity by looking at those also in the photo in addition to the candidate. Backdrops matter in photos.

It is critical that a launch take place in the correct order of communication. For example, you may wish to have a series of announcements going out at the same time or one minute after another through various forms of communication. Courtesy of the order of communications matters. Communicating to friends, family, your employer, your boss, your work colleagues and more must be done thoughtfully. The order that others receive the news matters and should be considered through the lens of those who may wonder why they received the news before or after others received the news. Public forums such as Twitter, Instagram, Facebook and YouTube should invariably be the last order of communication. Seldom would everything be simultaneous, because there is usually someone or some group who deserve a heads up that your news is forthcoming. That group may be your colleagues who you are serving with, your family or some other person who you need to be sensitive to. You need everyone's vote and caring about everyone matters.

Figure 8. *Campaign launch announcement*

> **Crouse for Mayor Campaign Kickoff Party**
> September 21st
> 5:00-8:00pm
> 7:00pm Official Kickoff
> St. Albert Community Hall on Perron Street
>
> •Bring entire family
> •Complimentary food & refreshments
> •Oilers game door prize

6.5 THE FACTORS THAT ALL ADD UP

After viewing many election campaigns in Canada, reading books on the subject and knocking on perhaps 50,000 doors, I have learned that there are many factors that go into the assessment of a candidate in a community.

I have determined some of the factors that matter the most, although the weighting on each depends on the community, the government order, the riding, the constituency, the ward or the region. It may depend on population, diversity, demographics, socioeconomic standards and more. There are many factors, and below some, listed in no particular order. Each item may have a different weighting than others and depends on so many factors. For example, name recognition in a community of 5,000 for a six-term incumbent, where there is no newspaper, will have a different weighting for a first-time candidate than it will for a candidate running in a community of 500,000.

While there is not one single silver bullet, door knocking separates many candidates from other candidates.

Below are some of the factors that influences the voters:

- Incumbent or not
- People the candidate knows personally
- Number of doors knocked on
- Far left and far right voters' vote
- Candidate visibility
- Age of the candidate
- Local newspaper independent views
- Education
- Platform
- Platform communication tactics
- The "lift" by other candidates with similar views
- The "lift" by the far left and far right
- The "lift" by radicals
- Campaign quality
- Newspaper articles volume
- Seen in the community
- Gender of the candidate
- Sweeping change being sought
- Forum performance
- Name recognition
- If the candidate seen as "anti-establishment"
- If the candidate seen as "pro-establishment"
- Business support

- Impact of candidate's spouse or partner
- Impact of candidate's parents
- Impact of candidate's children
- Website quality and availability
- Social media strategy
- Mail-outs or drop-offs
- Signage quality and numbers
- Signage size and location
- Government employee voter preferences
- Appearance and looks
- Negative campaigning effectiveness
- Positive campaigning effectiveness
- Last election carryover
- Colour appeal of materials
- Overall branding
- Appeal to seniors
- Appeal to non-seniors
- Popularity in the community
- History in the jurisdiction

6.6 SUBSEQUENT RALLIES OR EVENTS

Momentum must be maintained, and it is easy for momentum to be lost in many campaigns.

What a candidate is embarking upon is a "change" of sorts. In John P. Kotter's change management theory, he describes how important it is that when change is occurring (influencing voters' minds in this case) the change sponsor (the candidate in this case) must have a strategy in place to maintain momentum. Kotter describes maintaining momentum as one of eight steps to success.

That momentum may take shape in numerous ways. Examples of momentum boosters are regular events, frequent campaign team meetings, regular press releases, and regular updates to the public, mail-outs and more. Continuing to motivate the volunteers matters, because fatigue, burnout and even apathy may occur during a campaign period. The candidate may even begin to exhibit some of the same behaviours as the campaign workers or volunteers. All of these signal that the momentum is being lost, and it is important to schedule activities to ensure momentum is maintained. Pre-timed release of messages or pre-timed platform updates are only a couple of examples of approaches to keep the momentum. Mid-campaign rallies are another way. Announcing a new platform category also gets traction.

The size of the campaign and the volunteer capability are key factors in maintaining momentum. Loss of momentum is when the candidate must lead the way and demonstrate commitment, work ethic, visibility and support, and encourage the heart of everyone around them. Events or meetings are ways to do that.

CHAPTER 7
THE MESSAGE DELIVERY

7.1 THE PROFILE OF THE VOTER

THE PROFILE OF A TYPICAL VOTER IN elections may influence a candidate's election strategy, and indeed it should.

In a report from *Municipal World,* two members of staff at Brock University reported information that may assist in the development of a message delivery strategy. When asked in that survey by Joseph Kushner and David Siegel at Brock University (asked of both voters and non-voters), why people do not vote, the most frequent reasons were "apathy, lack of information, meaninglessness of their vote and electors simply being lazy."

When non-voters were asked why they did not vote, the most common reasons noted were "too busy, polling station problems and non-trustworthy candidates."

Understanding the profile of the modern-day voter may assist in establishing a strategy of message delivery by a candidate, and there are some basic elements to understand.

First, the voting turnout by age group in Canadian elections in recent years is as follows:

Age range	Turnout
18–24	26%
25–44	53%
45–64	71%
Over 65	79%

Education level attained has some effect on voter turnout, and the following data demonstrates that:

Level of education	Turnout
Primary	70%
Secondary	64%
University/College	62%
Postgraduate	62%

Income level of the voter has some effect on voter turnout, and the following data demonstrates that:

Level of income	Percent
Under $30,000	58%
$30,000–$50,000	60%
$50,000–$100,000	63%
Over $100,000	70%

Property ownership status of the voter has some effect on voter turnout, and the following data demonstrates that:

Property ownership voting:

Renters	51%
Homeowners	71%

Whether a voter is active in the community or politically has some effect on voter turnout, and the following data demonstrates that:

Political and community activeness of a voter:

Politically involved	75%
Not politically involved	58%
Community involved	70%
Not involved in community	60%

How long a voter has lived in a community has some effect on voter turnout, and the following data demonstrates that:

Years living in the local community where they are voting:

Less than 2 years	41%
2 to 10 years	59%
11 to 25 years	63%
More than 25 years	68%

While there are many deductions that may be made from this, there are no overwhelming statistics here that would cause one to ignore one demographic or target certain tactics to one category. The most compelling correlation is that between age and voter turnout.

It is due to the above statistics that a candidate must explore all options that are available to them, and it is also clearly a compelling reason to door knock, because it is very probable that there is a diversity of voters who answer doors. That diversity best reflects the groups covered in the above statistics collected by Brock University.

7.2 MAILING MATERIALS

Canada Post offers to perform mail-outs using a variety of approaches, and the cost of such delivery should be explored. The best-known mailing approach is using cardstock material, and it is suggested that the exact same material that is used as drop-off during door knocking is used as mail-out material. With such a high percentage of Canadians receiving mail through super mailbox outlets, if a campaign can afford mail-outs, this approach should be utilized. Whether the mail is read, tossed, or left on the dining room table for others to view, a mail-out makes its way into the hands of some percentage of voters, and a diverse type of voter.

If the mail-out material colours are eye catching or emotionally connecting, someone in a household may view it, read it, collect it or decide based on it. The last name visibility matters and must be clearly seen on a mail-out.

Canada Post offers delivery by postal code, which can be useful as you may wish to target an area of your jurisdiction that you are not able to get to or not able to door knock in for various reasons. Of course, there are islands, fly-in communities. Long-distance drives to commute to, and costs or time to visit those areas, are all factors. Bundling the right numbers up for the correct postal code locations allows you to target certain geographic areas. Doubling up with door knocking and mail-out cards further increases the chance of accessing someone different answering the door than the one picking up mail. Adding a drop-off at a door additionally increases the probability of the card being seen.

Bundling information for mail-out requirements and costs are available from Canada Post and should be explored.

7.3 RADIO

Radio advertisements are expensive but may be the best way to reach the voters in a particular community. Depending on how many radio stations may be accessed in a community, this may be a viable approach that is effective.

For example, a community in one area of the country may have only one – and very popular – radio station, and therefore it will be a reasonable alternative to advertising a message.

Radio messaging needs to be succinct and focus on the candidate's last name as the most important clip of a message. Keep any message on the radio simple. In radio advertising, the message is more about name recognition and less about the important campaign details that residents may not be prepared to listen to on the radio.

Radio interviews can be very important if you are able to set them up. If you include the radio station in your ongoing, public communications such as your launch announcement, there may be some appetite by the radio station to perform an interview. Similarly, a radio advertising salesperson may also have an appetite to arrange for a radio interview. This may be a legitimate quid pro quo as you are paying for a service and perhaps can negotiate a free interview as part of an advertising agreement.

7.4 TELEVISION

Television (and radio) advertising is more often reserved for national and provincial parties, but it depends on the jurisdiction. Parties have a need to reach more, further and wider, than local candidates. The ability to raise funds to afford television advertising is also a factor and is perhaps the most important factor.

With the number of television stations available to the average viewer, television advertising may not be worth the money spent, and therefore is primarily used only by parties, premiers or party leaders at the national party level.

In the 2015 Alberta provincial election, the far-right party (Wildrose) stated that their goal was to become the official opposition to the centre-right party (Conservatives). The leader of the left-leaning party, (NDP) Rachel Notley, and indeed the underdog, stated on television that her goal was to become premier. Messaging and goal setting matters, and with the television audience keen in 2015 for politics, she knew how to use the airtime. The NDP party won a majority in perhaps one of the most surprising elections in Alberta's history. Television played a big part in that, including a televised debate, believed by many to be a game changer.

7.5 NEWSPAPERS

Newspapers continue to be well read in many communities and community newspapers cover regional, local, municipal, school board, First Nations and aboriginal community elections. Candidates are generally willing and able to spend funds to perform some local advertising, and there are many tactics and approaches that candidates should consider in this regard.

Candidates should request an editorial board meeting as most candidates may not think of this. This is an interview with key newspaper reporters, and it may assist you in delivering or launching your message. Newspapers may actually unintentionally migrate to help those candidates who are working to make the reporters' jobs the easier (knowingly or unknowingly. This slant in reporting occurs with reporters because the reporters have so little time to penetrate some stories or research some candidates.

Advertising in colour is more effective and expensive than black-and-white advertising, but if the candidate is able to afford it, branding and image are deepened with colour.

Locations of the advertisements within the newspaper and location upon the pages themselves may cost differently as reading patterns dictate where readers look to first when they browse or look at any given page. Page three of a newspaper is a prime advertising spot for candidates since page three is a widely viewed page in a community newspaper, as an example.

Inside the front cover page of a newspaper is also an important location, and if the campaign can afford it, that is a good page to purchase in its entirety.

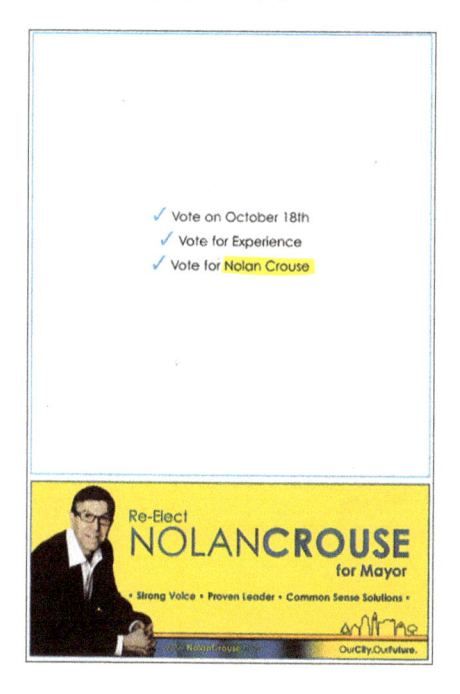

Figure 9. *Full page newspaper advertisement*

The campaign must determine which newspapers in a cycle to advertise the most in. The second last and last newspapers before an election date are important, depending on the date that the newspaper comes to the homes or the date the newspaper is available to the public. For example, a newspaper arriving on Election Day may not get seen. A newspaper that is mailed out through Canada Post may take two or three days to arrive and may not get picked up or read before an election. This intelligence gathering can be done weeks before any election. The sooner this intelligence is gathered, the more time it gives the campaign to book the choice spots and target newspaper advertising to when it will have maximum value. Daily, bi-weekly and weekly newspapers all have different cycles and distribution networks and this needs research.

Some campaigns attempt to fill out space in a newspaper advertisement with substantial, small-font information. One must remember that first and foremost, elections are about name recognition, and secondly, about the message. Party advertising may wish to keep things even more simple as the key need is the logo, the brand, the leader's name and where to locate the platform or policy positions online. Local campaigns have more local needs when it comes to newspaper advertising.

Any opportunity to perform interviews or answer questions posted or posed by a local newspaper reporter should be capitalized on. This is an opportunity for free space and free name recognition. Answering such questions for information by a reporter must be prioritized as important. The public frowns upon anyone who has "no comment," or "not available for comment," or "did not reply to this questionnaire" next to their name. The public is watching and making judgments based on a variety of things; being a fair communicator with the media is critical, and communication works both ways.

When I was involved in a baseball league, I spoke with the local sportswriter about what he writes about. He shared that since he is not able to get to every ball game in town, he relies on the coaches who provide him information and he rewards them by writing about their games, even though they might not be the most important games played in the league that night. His words were simple when he shared: "the squeaky wheel gets the grease." It may have been the first time I had ever heard that phrase, but it stuck with me the rest of my life, and in the media, it clearly holds true.

For those communities that rely heavily on newspapers, it is important that candidates ensure they are working to increase name recognition plus communicating with the voting public. Voters need to get to know more about you, and it stands to reason that the number of votes one gets may be somewhat proportional to the coverage (size and number) of advertisements one takes out. Statistical analyses that I have performed bears that out, and advertising through a newspaper needs strong consideration. Because of this, quality, location, colour, size and branding matter. Money raised for this purpose is important for the four weeks leading up to an election, and if funds are short, target the advertisements for the last week leading up to an election.

Research at a local library might assist in determining what some effective advertisements from previous campaigns looked like, which may even be evaluated in comparison to the top finishers in that election. Of course, parties who run advertisements may dictate branding and messaging, but for all other candidates wishing to advertise, a thorough review of election history in your community is advised.

For incumbents, there is a lot of benefit to newspaper coverage between elections. I performed a comprehensive analysis of the number of individual name mentions of an entire council, by member, between elections. The two candidates who were discussed and quoted the most in the local newspaper (including criticism and bad news) also received the most votes the subsequent election. That data reinforces the need for politicians to be active with the media. Someone whom I admire and studied a lot, William Edwards Deming, would often say, "How else would they know?" The same goes in advertising, business and politics. If the information is not getting to others, how else would they know?

As advanced voting becomes more and more common, as mail-in ballots become more and more common, some of this data will shift and should be considered in getting the message out and encouraging the voters to vote. Newspaper usage and availability is also changing significantly and is slowly becoming less relevant in many communities.

Figure 10. *Example of a newspaper advertisement*

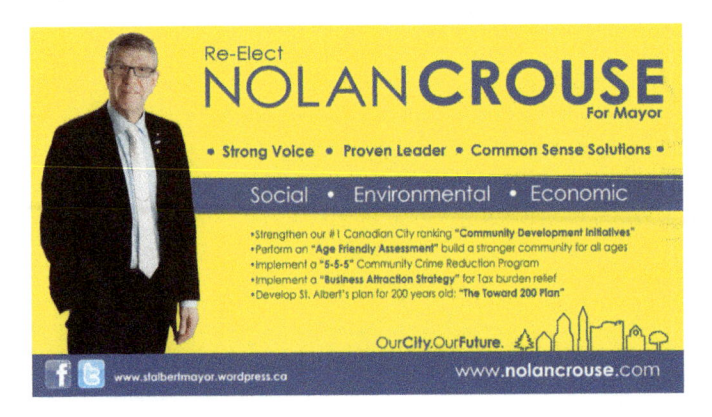

Figure 11. *Example of a newspaper advertisement*

7.6 MAGAZINES

Magazines may be an opportunity for advertising but generally are expensive, and magazines are typically published less frequently than is needed for election cycles. There may be some opportunities with some magazines that are able to communicate ideological messages over a four- or eight-week span for a political party.

Magazine advertising is generally not of high value because of the readership, distribution and timing of when magazine readers actually read the magazine itself.

7.7 FORUMS AND PUBLIC SPEAKING OPPORTUNITIES

There are many forums to assist with messaging, name recognition and sharing with the public your message and your brand.

One type of forum might be an online chat opportunity that allows for asynchronous (pre-recorded messages plus permitting responses) or synchronous (live) chats. Posting information on Facebook forums is one example of an effective forum strategy. During a campaign, one should seek these opportunities. Avoid lengthy debate or conversation over any particular topic, but demonstrating interest is an important tactic for name recognition and messaging.

Live online forums may also be conducted at any time of day or night as viewers may choose to engage, listen or not, but an online communication opportunity is useful to have in the evenings when it is too late for door knocking or too late for meetings.

There may be blogs and websites and chat sites that come to your attention, and it is wise to briefly engage as much as possible in such sites. While the sites may be self-serving to those who are on that site or owned by special interest groups, remember you are representing all constituents in your riding or community and whether others agree with you or whether others disagree with you is often irrelevant during a campaign period.

There are special interest groups that form online during election times. It is common for these forums to take a position and then look for candidates who will support their special interest. The special interest may be to join together to find candidates who will support a new library, support a cause, support a new facility or support funding of an initiative. Candidates who are seeking office should engage and not make any promises that are not able to be met. You can always take a position online that you will consider all input once elected because you must assess all views on any particular topic.

There are live, in-person forums where voters are looking for candidates to differentiate themselves from others. Such live forums are usually seen as critical for candidates to attend, as the attendance and views are scrutinized by many, and the word spreads substantially following such forums. Many attendees are looking to see how candidates handle controversy, questions, pressure, speaking opportunities, and how they represent their ideology or their views. Some attendees, of course, are looking for a "train wreck" to see how the candidates handle themselves under pressure of controversy and scrutiny. Any forum or speech opportunity must be capitalized upon. There will be numerous opportunities to deliver a message, and all opportunities provided must be used unless there are compelling reasons to do otherwise. When planning any timed speeches, plan your speeches at 2.5 words per second so that you are able to get your entire speech completed within the allocated time frames. Speak for less and not more than your allotted time.

If you have an opportunity to speak at public forums, if there is an audience, having planted questions by your supporters, visible signage and pre-planned cheering by your supporters are tactical advantages that experienced campaigns know the benefits of. Candidates or campaign workers should arrive at all such opportunities to speak well in advance of any other candidates if there are multiple candidates. Workers and volunteers should set up in the most visible locations. Campaigns should consider setting up signage, door knocking cards, buttons, bumper stickers, car window flags, business cards and other materials so they are highly visible and available for attendees if the opportunity presents itself.

If you are requested to come to a particular location alone to speak with an organization or group, some of the same principles apply in that it is not common that everyone in that particular forum may know your name, what you stand for or much about you, and therefore, supplying attendees with information is critical to spreading the word. Usually, any voter attending these types of forums understands what they are there for and expects information to be provided to them to make an informed decision. Have handouts ready if the circumstances warrants such effort.

When asked a question at any forum, ensure you understand the question, because there are many nuances and idiosyncrasies about questions. It is important to use all your listening and clarification abilities to demonstrate a variety of listening skills that you have learned in your life. Learn to communicate quickly, succinctly, and with soundbites in the time allotment in way that leaves clarity. Always ensure others are made aware of your last name.

During organized multi-candidate campaign events, candidates are invariably provided opportunities to speak, introduce themselves, share their platform or party information or provide closing remarks on a topic. In the appendix, there are examples of opening and closing speeches to illustrate the succinct nature of such messaging, where every word needs to count. As an example, speaking at a rate of 2.5 words per second, and provided 60 seconds to open or close an argument or provide an introduction, means keeping on point, on message and on time.

Bring extra copies of any speech with you and give a copy to anyone who wants a copy. Email that same speech to yourself in case you forget to bring the speech and email it to anyone who wishes to have a copy. Your speech needs to be public property.

7.8 EMAILS

Someone needs to ensure that emails related to your campaign are monitored and answered during a campaign period. Sometimes specific email addresses are set up for the purposes of an election only, and then are not monitored or answered. Other times emails are not answered by candidates because of time pressures to get to all the correspondence that may arrive during an election campaign.

I have always maintained that during an election campaign all emails should get addressed late at night or early in the morning. There are a couple of reasons for that approach. First, and most importantly the emails must get answered. Second, answering late at night will likely mean that there will not be an immediate response back. Late and early emails reduce the probability of creating a lengthy email exchange that may not be a good use of time. Third, daytime activities can be dedicated to matters that can only occur during the day, such as face-to-face interaction (meetings and door knocking). Finally, the public who are seeking information via email will see that you are prepared to work late at night or early in the morning and will therefore respect your commitment.

Answer emails.

7.9 WEBSITE

Have a website and track the traffic.

The name of the website should include your last name in some fashion. If it can be as simple as your first and last name, which allows for simplicity, ease of understanding and locating the site. Be aware that it is common for others to attempt to reserve the natural domain name(s) that you may wish to personally choose for your website. For that reason, the booking of a domain name is one of those early booking activities that needs to be completed. You and your campaign team need to decide how many domain names to book, and for how long.

Use every tool that is available with today's technology to drive traffic to your website. Ask your volunteers to tag your website and include tags and links in all the campaign Twitter, Instagram, Facebook and LinkedIn accounts, as well as Google Drives, brochures, press releases and any other media forum to drive traffic to your website.

Include the website address (imbedded) in your signature on all emails.

Use your website as a full depository of all information from your campaign, and anything that can be public should be included on the website.

Have a short video on your website introducing yourself.

Always request from your supporters, community leaders, colleagues and community members comments that can be seen as endorsements of you as a legitimate and supported candidate. Post these on your website. Attempt to obtain quotes from individuals whom many would know in the community or within your electorate and whose voices might be viewed as a good endorsement. Be prepared to send to some people your proposed endorsement wording and allow them to simply say "yes," or allow them to change it. This is the easiest to do for most. Post all the endorsements that you have permission to post on your website.

Since names of donors are at times sensitive, it is best to name donors exactly as per the legal disclosure schedule. Do not include the names of donors on a website or in a blog.

Include no gimmicks, distractions, movement or difficult tactics on or inside your website. Keep it simple and branded with your chosen colours and slogans. Have simple tabs to make it easy for anyone to navigate through the website.

Keep the website simple, include lots of photos and most importantly, ensure your last name is on the main page in large font.

Allow your website to be translated easily with a language translate tab built into the website functions.

Ensure there is an easy way to contact the candidate or campaign team built into the website.

Ensure your website offers easy ways to volunteer, request information, become a lawn sign host or other ways for a visitor to offer assistance.

Ensure there is an easy way on the website to donate to the campaign either cash or gifts in kind.

It is wise to pay for the domain for several years so that it can be used in future years for various purposes, including running for re-election.

Have marketing and branding experts use every tool that you can afford to drive traffic to all your online sites, including your website.

7.10 FACEBOOK

Facebook conversations, forums and postings are a must for several reasons. The majority of people who see your posting may be supporters, so you remind them that you are involved in a campaign, something they may not be aware of. Many will likely vote for you if they are in your voting district. Have your page be clear that you are running for elected office.

Posting additional information on your Facebook feed allows others to like, share, comment on, tag others and more. The multiplier effect cannot be underestimated.

THE POLITICAL CAMPAIGN "HOW-TO" GUIDE

Always tag others and post a lot during a campaign.

Facebook is a branding opportunity for demonstrating your brand and your beliefs. Use your colours, photos and slogan as much as you can on Facebook once you publicly announce your intention to seek office.

Advertising opportunities are easily available on Facebook and other media platforms and should be explored. If a campaign has funds to use this advertising approach, it should be explored and used. Driving traffic to hear about what you have to say and who you are is an approach that paid advertising through Facebook will assist with. Your Facebook pages are an opportunity to drive traffic to your website to browse, learn more, donate or otherwise assist.

Take time to find new friends who are in your sphere of friendship, community and potential followers. There is a well-shared theory of "six degrees of separation," and certainly increasing Facebook friends is one of those ways to increase reach of your message.

Figure 12. *Facebook page screenshot*

7.11 TWITTER, INSTAGRAM AND OTHER

Use every tool possible to communicate, gain support and ensure voters vote for you or know who you are including using common social media platforms such as Twitter, Instagram and other such platforms. Voters need to hear from candidates and delivering the message may mean an increased use of these platforms before, during and following an election. Whether it is simply for name recognition, partisan party information, constituency information, platform dissemination, advanced voting schedule or polling station information, all such tools should be explored and used.

Different individuals, different demographics and different groups use different approaches to obtain information about news, sports and politics. Like many aspects of an election campaign, while there is some research as to preferences and tendencies of different genders, ages and other demographics, one simply never knows what avenue someone may use Therefore, it is critical to maximize the number of options you have to deliver your message. It may even be simply that you need to increase your name recognition, especially if you are a relatively unknown individual seeking office.

One tactic to gain followers is to follow and be linked to many individuals in your constituency. Often if you follow others, they will follow you, and if you plan to run, the sooner you take the time to increase your number of followers, the better. Since your objective is to maximize the number who are seeing your message, you need to work at your reach. You can increase your reach two-to four-fold with significant social media action and a significant increase in who you interact with because of the multiplier effect of such connections. Remember, traditional newspaper advertising is becoming less effective in many communities because of declining readership, and social media platforms are critical to you being better known.

7.12 LINKEDIN

LinkedIn posts are a must for several reasons. The majority of people who see your LinkedIn posts, like on Facebook, are your connections of some sort, and by posting you remind them that you are involved in a campaign. Like on Facebook, many individuals may not be aware of your involvement in seeking office or may not be aware of your views, and therefore you need to use the platform.

Like Facebook, posting allows others to like, share, comment and more. The multiplier effect cannot be underestimated. LinkedIn also has a demographic that may or may not overlap with Facebook. LinkedIn is also less political in nature than Facebook and one would need to be more measured with the LinkedIn posts.

Always tag others and post more than normal during a campaign. Due to the nature of LinkedIn posts, this is an opportunity to share very complex and cerebral postings and is simply another avenue to convey messages as to why others should support you in your quest to serve in a public office.

Finally, LinkedIn is also an opportunity for demonstrating your brand, ideas and beliefs. Use your chosen colours, photos and slogans as much as you can on LinkedIn during this time. Additionally, use LinkedIn to drive traffic to your website and other social media platforms.

7.13 LETTERS TO THE EDITOR OR COLUMNS

Some newspapers do not permit letters to the newspaper editor during election campaigns, while other newspapers encourage it, believing that it is in the public's best interest to learn as much as possible about candidates.

If permitted, candidates should use this opportunity; if not permitted, if the newspaper is willing to publish letters from supporters, those writers should be encouraged to submit important supportive letters. Using any and all endorsements is wise. Names on these letters are also critical, as anonymous letters are less credible, may not get published, can be viewed quite skeptically and may be ineffective.

Many candidates begin writing letters to newspaper editors and op-eds before declaring any plans to become a candidate. This is an equally good way to gain visibility or name recognition and is a wise tactic. Ensure any messaging is appropriate, and ensure the letters are well written because they form the digital (and paper) footprint of an individual.

It may also be of interest to a newspaper for a candidate to request a regular column spot. This is particularly effective for an elected candidate who has a regular message to deliver throughout their time as an elected official. This may or may not be permitted to continue throughout an election campaign. For example, a mayor, chief, reeve, MLA or MP holding office may wish to publish an ongoing column for years, and the campaign is simply another opportunity to add to it. If the newspaper chooses to pause this process, that incumbent has already gained an advantage for several years in communicating their message to the public thereby increasing their name recognition and delivering important messaging.

7.14 DOOR DROPS

Door drops are a card that you drop off at someone's home door without actually door knocking. Door drops are one critical approach to delivering a message. The strategy for door knocking is covered in the next chapter. It is best for the door drop material to be similar or identical to the door knocking material, however.

Door drops are best if sized at 9.3 cm (3.67 in) x 21.6 cm (8.5 in) and printed on cardstock with a weight of 14 pt. or 16 pt. This size has many distinct advantages that cannot be underestimated and are as follows:

1. Small enough to be flexible
2. Small enough to be able to carry easily in hands or pouches
3. Large enough to deliver a message
4. Less costly, as three door knocking cards can be printed and cut from a standard sheet of cardstock (known as 8.5 x 11 in)
5. Easily obtained in all colour options
6. Easy to stand it up in a mailbox at a home
7. Easily slid into a doorjamb that is not open
8. Stiff enough and large enough to withstand all handling processes
9. Easily mailed
10. Good for door knocking material and can be sent by email too

It will take a team of volunteers to either mail materials, door knock or door drop, and each strategy can be employed and even doubled up over a campaign period if a campaign can afford more than one option of delivery. A heavily rural area may benefit by having materials mailed to houses, and a heavily urban area may benefit the most by having materials dropped off, mailed, or provided via door knocking (or all three).

One tactic *not* to undertake is to perform door drops at high speed by dropping a brochure off, ringing the doorbell and moving quickly to the next drop-off. This is inappropriate, and while it may get a percentage of people coming to the door, this "hit and run" approach with the hope that someone will answer the door and see the drop-off is tacky and should not be used as a tactic. Do not ring the doorbell unless you are prepared to chat.

To assist your door drop volunteers, include a street map, chart and a bag with the door drops in them for each volunteer so they are clear on the area to cover.

THE POLITICAL CAMPAIGN "HOW-TO" GUIDE

Figure 13. *Door drop and door knocking card*

Figure 14. *Door drop card and coloured plastic bag*

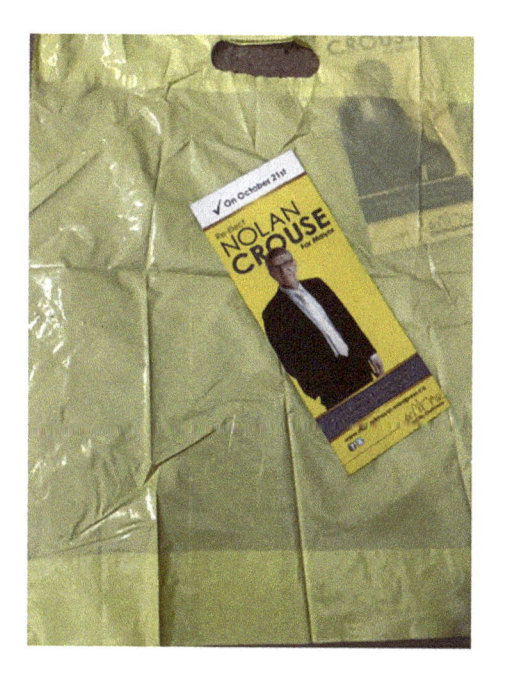

Figure 15. *Door drop plan*

Neighbourhood	Zone	Amount	Map	Volunteer	Phone	Email	Volunteer Address	Assigned	Bagged	Delivered	Dropped
Sir John Area	1	150	Yes	Mark							
	2	145	Yes	Cheryl							
	3	135	Yes	Judy							
	4	150	Yes								
	5	200	Yes								
	6	225	Yes	Roger							
	7	130	Yes	Maggie							
	Total	1135									
Pierre Hill	1	150	Yes	Leslie							
	2	125	No								
	3	140	No	Ken							
	Total	415									
Dion Subdivision	1	185	No	Dale							
	2	145	No								
	3	135	No								
	4	115	No	Chuck							
	5	160	No	Chuck							

Figure 16. *Door drop tracking*

Brochure drop-off

#	Last Name	First Name	Street Drop	City	PC	Helper	# Drops	Phone	email
1	Adamson	Jill	Brook Street	Johnstown	T8N5T9	Jake Jones	38	555-555-5555	Jill@jilladamson.com
2	Roberts	Bob	Dean Street	Johnstown	T8N5T9	Kate Askin	58	555-555-9999	Bob@bobroberts.com
3									
4									
5									
6									
7									
8									
9									
10									
11									
12									
13									
14									
15									
16									

7.15 PHONING

It is critical that some phoning occurs during campaign periods if the campaign team is provided a voter or membership list. This approach is most common in Canada for party politics where the names and numbers of the residents, member lists or voting lists are available. This is less often available for local campaigns in much of Canada.

It is common for many campaign volunteers prefer to work from their own homes. Some are unable to drive, are homebound or are not physically mobile and prefer phoning as their approach to campaigning. If a campaign team can provide phone crews or individuals with lists of names and phone numbers, there is substantial influence with direct phone calls.

Of course, there may also be follow-up phone calls that are significant to make on election days. There is a need for some members of the public to be reminded to get out and vote or a need to give voters directions to a polling station. It is also an opportunity for some voters to seek a ride, information about the candidate and information about the hours of the polling station.

If phoning occurs well in advance of the election, there may be an opportunity to communicate information such as mail-in ballot procedures or advanced polling information, just to name a couple of possibilities.

Critical in all phoning is that the workers identify themselves and ensure it is crystal clear which candidate the volunteer is phoning on behalf of, with clarity on the candidate's last name in every phone call.

Candidates should also change their voice mails on their personal cell phone and home phone to reflect their plan as a candidate.

7.16 ROBOCALLS AND TEXTING

Robocalls and mass texting are often not welcomed, because of the number of scam calls and other unwelcome phoning or texting that regularly may occur. The use of a system that calls numerous numbers seeking funds and candidate support is less prevalent today and I would fully discourage this approach. Permission of phone calling is now much more regulated than in past years.

Federal, provincial and territorial legislation is ever-evolving relative to access to home phone numbers, mobile numbers and work numbers. This must be carefully assessed before such a contact approach is utilized for campaigning.

7.17 PRESS RELEASES

Press releases are a legitimate approach to announcing information at the beginning and midstream of any election campaign. The press itself will determine if a press release is newsworthy enough to do an article on, written by a journalist. However, campaigns are free to make and release mid-campaign announcements or press releases at any time. The title "press release" provides some credibility and can be posted on websites, social media, blogs and other locations where the words "press release" garner some attention.

Issuance of press releases is a campaign strategy that is effective for national, provincial and territorial campaigns where the parent party has new information that may not have been disclosed or originally contained within previous campaign material or in platform material.

Press releases are also an opportunity to respond to an opposition candidate, as this can be an opportunity to address rumours or misinformation.

Any endorsements that you are able to include in a press release should be included. It is always wise to quote the candidate so that the candidate is accountable for what is being stated within a press release. Any generic statements will not be as credible and may not be reported by the mainstream press reporters.

7.18 GOOGLE AND YOUTUBE

Google and YouTube are important for today's campaigns. Online user traffic tracking, and trends of such traffic, can be used to the advantage of any campaign advertising strategies established based on such traffic. While these patterns are best understood by the technical members of your campaign team, the data can reinforce a few things.

First, having campaign members who are technically savvy in the area of patterns of online traffic will maximize your coverage online. Second, a campaign that can afford some online traffic assessment and which is able to apply that knowledge will gain advantages over those candidates who do not involve these analytical approaches.

A campaign or a candidate should consider having a YouTube channel and using YouTube to communicate messages. As is noted in this chapter, it is necessary to use many approaches to communicating messages, and YouTube is one more approach to consider.

Paid advertising embedded in YouTube or using YouTube videos to communicate messaging are all options that increase your outreach, and consequently, Google and YouTube use can have significant advantages for a candidate, a party or a campaign. For example, preparing video of a candidate door knocking and posting on YouTube is a good way to communicate progress, as long as traffic is driven to the YouTube channel.

7.19 INFORMAL VENUES

Every area of Canada has informal approaches to reaching a voter, and this should be explored. It can be called "the coffee shop phenomenon," as this phenomenon exists in every corner of Canada. There are many adults and seniors who gather for coffee in Tim Hortons, there are neighbours who gather at block parties, there are friends who gather at restaurants, and there are farmers who gather when the weather does not permit other farming activities to take place. Knowing where those groups gather can help candidates plan daytime destinations to go to.

For example, if you are aware that a group of fishing friends gather in Nova Scotia for a regular social event in a public place, it is an area to stop in and chat with that group. We often see the candidates on television at a coffee shop, having a chat and shaking hands, and this is welcome by most. First, you are meeting people "on their turf," and within a group some are bold enough to ask questions or challenge a candidate. The numbers of 5:1 or 10:1 can be intimidating for some candidates, and many candidates avoid such groups, but it is also an opportunity to communicate, answer a lingering question, become known, listen to the views or simply meet some people you had not ever met. You can even pick up the tab for the coffee! I visited countless groups such as these and I was always welcome and seldom sat down or paid the tab, but the opportunities are endless.

These informal gatherings take place at swimming pool coffee shops, at the legions, at recreation centres, at malls and at restaurants. The list of locations and numbers of attendees are a lot. It is a form of door knocking that has tremendous value to those who are willing to engage in this fashion. It is not always for the faint of heart, frankly speaking, for a candidate or party representative who may need to be prepared for a difficult conversation.

During election campaigns, consider being available at other numerous (especially public) gathering places and events that you may not normally frequent. This might include a bus stop, an arena, a swimming pool, hockey tryouts, ringette games, curling clubs, museums, art galleries, seniors' lodges, recreation centres, ball diamonds, rugby games, soccer fields and cricket pitches.

It is also wise to attend services at places of worship, and while you may be a stranger in some, the tactic can be valuable if handled professionally and discretely. Handing out brochures at a funeral or church service is an example of unacceptable campaigning that has significant negative consequences, and rightfully so. I recall two candidates attending a funeral with their campaign badges on and who were heavily criticized on social media for such tactless campaigning.

Many high school students and post-secondary students vote, and if not, students certainly influence voters. Consider a youth and a student plan, and interaction with students can be a formal or informal interaction. Some schools welcome this.

One more thing: regardless of the gathering, before one goes out campaigning to any venue, it is wise to floss one's teeth!

7.20 BLOGS, RECORDINGS AND PODCASTS

While it is a time-consuming process, another tool used by candidates or campaigns is writing and posting blogs. Some candidates will have numerous pre-written blogs, while others may blog each day on how their campaign is proceeding. Others will have bloggers on their campaign team. These are all good approaches.

Some candidates will have someone blog about the campaign progress, candidate thoughts, door knocking progress and more. Like any other communication mechanism, these also work as long as traffic is driven to the blog site.

In 2013, the number of views (hits) on my blog site was about double the number of hits on my website.

It is also very easy to perform recordings throughout a campaign, and of course, prior to a campaign period. With access to platforms like Zoom, recording campaign information, thoughts, interviews and blogging is common and encouraged. Posting such information on various communication channels such as YouTube, Facebook, Twitter, LinkedIn and your website that assists others in gaining knowledge and insight about the issues, the party, the platform and the candidate. The sharing of your media links by your followers adds to the campaign success.

Verbal endorsements from others during any such recordings assist in credibility, help validate the legitimacy of a candidate and is encouraged.

The process of driving traffic to websites, posting blogs and posting to other platforms has been discussed, and it needs to be taken seriously. Again, if you have the expertise to do so, it is critical to use all that expertise. If you do not have that skill yourself, it is wise to have someone on your team with the expertise to do this activity.

You may also choose to have a podcast series where you develop a platform, a theme, then record and publish a series of information views, opinions, knowledge, and wisdom to demonstrate to others your depth and breadth of knowledge about issues. Relevant topics or perhaps even a podcast that is unrelated to being an elected official helps offer insights that can assist with you building your brand and your followers.

7.21 LAWN SIGNS

There are three key elements to name recognition that lawn signs are important for. First, a lawn sign is an endorsement by one person for either a party or a candidate, and others see and view the person on that lawn sign as someone that they may like to vote for. Seeing someone in your neighbourhood endorsing a cause, a party or candidate may influence you, and that is the basis for one important reason for a lawn sign campaign.

Equally important to endorsement is that of name recognition. Seeing the name of a person on a lawn sign over and over again as a voter drives to and from work, goes shopping or walks past that sign, helps that name "stick" in their minds. This name can therefore be more easily recalled when at the ballot box. Name recognition permits the name to be repeated to others, discussed, researched and questioned. As such, the lawn sign offers that significant recollection benefit for a voter.

Third, the name of the person on the lawn sign becomes a trigger for intelligence gathering. Seeing a lawn sign with a name on a neighbour's lawn may cause you to check the Facebook page, the Twitter account or perform research such as through Google on that candidate for various reasons. The more lawn signs that a candidate has out and about, the more often research may be done on a candidate and the more potential there is for a vote for that name at the ballot box. That results in more potential that someone retweets, reposts or shares information and knowledge about that candidate.

When I was door knocking, I came across someone who had six lawn signs for seven vacant council spots, and the woman who answered the door asked me if I would put a lawn sign up on her lawn. She was a stranger to me, but she stated that she was going to support the first seven who knocked on her door. She viewed door knocking as hard work and believed that those who came to her door deserved her public endorsement. I quickly posted a lawn sign on her lawn.

It is important to have a plan for lawn signs after the election, such as picking all signs up, together with a proper location for drop-off. Additionally, a washing and storage plan needs to be considered.

Figure 17. *Lawn sign example*

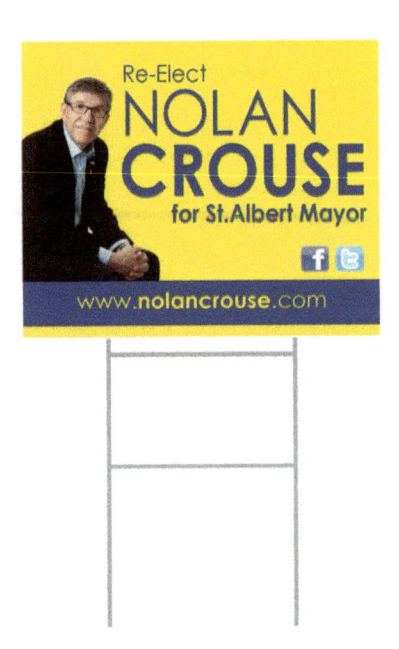

In the appendix is an example of a letter with instructions to any host of a lawn sign as to what to do with that sign after the election is completed.

7.22 STREET SIGNS

Street signs are a highly effective method of communicating to the public. They may be located on public or private property, depending on the jurisdiction. The eligibility of their location may be already established by a number of legal frameworks such as legislation, bylaws or policy. Given the public property nature, local safety, weather and traffic matters, the use and location of street signs must be carefully thought through. Additionally, there are significant potential issues such as vandalism, theft and damage to consider for those street signs on public property – more issues that private locations do not have.

There are usually traffic-related requirements of size and location of street signs that do not apply to lawn signs on private property, and it is incumbent upon the candidate to understand where street signs may be placed. For example, distance from intersections, blocking views of businesses, private property infringement or distance from traffic control devices are all considerations.

Many in your community have used street signs, and you would be wise to check with others for tips and advice. There are portable sign companies to rent from, or there perhaps are sign structures that you can borrow or purchase that can be adapted. Perhaps your local Kinsmen Club has signs used to advertise a fundraiser or an event and that organization has a battery of blank ones that you could borrow, repair afterwards and perhaps donate some funds to their club for the rental thereof. Many community groups and organizations use signs that are already constructed and built such that they can stand the test of time and weather. Many are already equipped with stakes or removable panels.

It is important to have a plan for street signs after the election. Picking all signs up, with a proper location for drop-off plus a washing and storage plan needs to be considered.

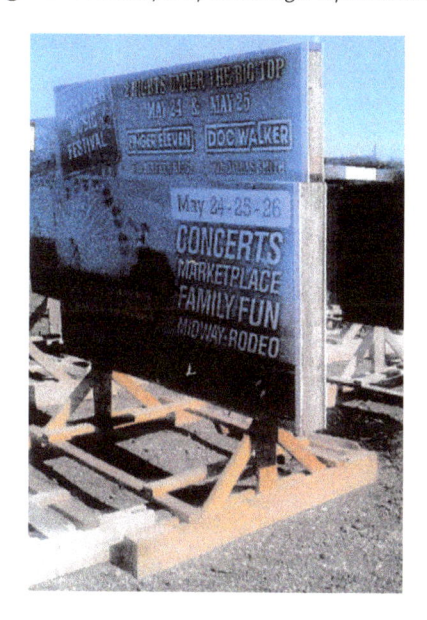

Figure 18. *Example of street sign infrastructure*

Compliments of the Kinsmen Club of St. Albert, Alberta
Used in election campaigns 2004, 2007, 2010, 2013

7.23 LAWN SIGN AND STREET SIGN DESIGN

The design of and approach to installation of lawn signs is important to plan for. Most lawn signs are manufactured using coroplast material with ribs running through the material. Below are some tips on how to design and install lawn signs.

Lawn signs (plus same size street signs)

1. Lawn sign material should not be paper and should be coroplast or plastic.
2. Lawn sign material thickness should be standard coroplast thickness gauge.
3. If using wooden stakes, the ribs need to run at 90 degrees to the stakes to ensure it does not bend in the wind.
4. If using double-pronged metal stakes as per the photo earlier in this chapter, the coroplast ribs need to run parallel to the stakes to allow the wires to be inserted.
5. The largest print on the lawn sign must be the candidate's last name.
6. The smaller print on the sign should be the candidate's first name.
7. Small street signs should have a small photo.
8. The colour of the coroplast must match the branded colours of the entire campaign.
9. Both sides of the coroplast should have identical writing so that it can be seen while travelling from either direction.
10. Lawn signs must be posted facing traffic.
11. Lawn signs must be visible near the front of a lawn and not within human touching from a sidewalk if possible.
12. Lawn signs must not interfere with any underground infrastructure such as sprinklers or valves.
13. Contrast of colors plus font size must be considered so that a driver can see the name at a glance.
14. The sign size should be such that the maximum number can be cut out of the traditional 48 x 96 inch material (4 x 8 panels).
15. Lawn sign dimensions should always be 24 inches or two feet wide.

The design and approach to installation of street signs is important because of many factors, including wind and other weather-related matters. Most larger street signs are manufactured using wooden materials and should be installed by qualified workers who understand the importance of weather, safety, location, sizing and legal requirements. Below are some tips on how to design and install street signs.

THE POLITICAL CAMPAIGN "HOW-TO" GUIDE

Street signs (larger than the 24-inch-wide lawn sign)

1. Street sign material should not be paper but can be lumber or plastic.
2. Street sign material thickness should be coroplast thickness gauge with stiff backing such as 3/8 inch thick wooden panels.
3. If using wooden stakes, the ribs need to run at 90 degrees to the stakes to ensure it does not bend in windy weather.
4. If using double-pronged metal stakes, the ribs need to run parallel to the stakes to allow the metal stakes to be inserted.
5. All street signs greater than 24 inches wide should be anchored well into the ground to avoid being windblown.
6. The largest print on the sign must be the candidate's last name.
7. The smaller print on the sign should be the candidate's first name.
8. Large street signs should have a large photo.
9. The colour of the signage must match the branded colours of the entire campaign.
10. Where possible, have the same writing on both sides of the sign so that it can be seen while travelling from either direction.
11. Signs must be posted in a location that makes them visible to traffic travelling in both directions.
12. Contrast of colors and font size must be large and clear so that a driver can see the name at a glance.

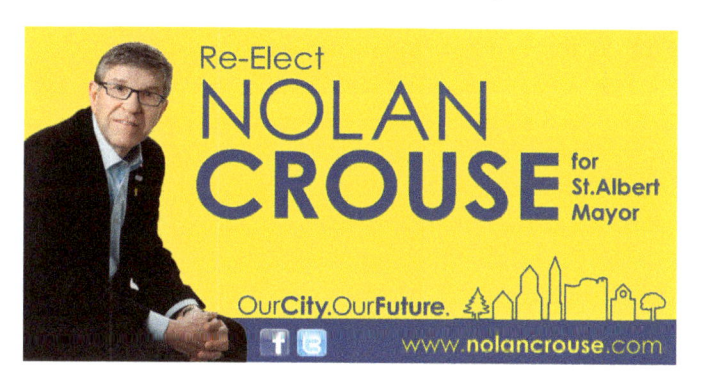

Figure 19. *48 x 96 inch Street sign*

Lawn sign and street sign recovery after an election is usually about 80%, since signs become damaged, lost or blown away.

7.24 BILLBOARDS

Billboards have the same effect that street signs do, with a few differences.

Billboards are substantially more expensive, and the location and impact of the messaging needs to be carefully thought out because of such expense.

Billboards must be booked months and even years in advance of an election.

Billboards may be electronic; therefore, the cycle time of one advertisement is usually quick. Increasing the cycle time and visibility may be able to be purchased from the supplier to increase frequency and visibility.

Billboards usually have a wider audience due to their highly travelled location and prominence. Traffic counts matter for both billboards and street signs, but since billboards are expensive, the billboard infrastructure is usually set up in high-traffic locations.

Billboards do not generally have any special legislative requirements like many other signage matters do.

Billboards require minimal installation and maintenance by the election team.

Billboards are seen mostly by vehicular traffic; consequently, the potential that billboards are not visible to many is significant.

Figure 20. *Billboard example*

7.25 CAMPAIGN OFFICE

A campaign office may be seen as a luxury, but it offers some advantages such as a place for storage, a gathering place for volunteers and perhaps a gathering place for the day and night of the election. Things that are important to ensure are available or taken care of in an election office are as follows:

- Staffing schedule
- Chairs
- Tables
- Computer
- Printer
- Whiteboard

- Banner (with your name)
- Tacks
- Cleaning schedule
- Garbage cans
- Photocopier
- Supplies
- Food
- Keys
- Power
- Phones
- Fax machine
- Fridge

7.26 OTHER VISUALS AND INFRASTRUCTURE

There is a never-ending abundance of other visuals and infrastructure that can be seen as valuable to deliver messaging for candidate name recognition.

There are lens cloths, pens, lighters, flags, pins, mugs, water bottles, vehicle window flags and many other trinkets and techniques that are creatively used by candidates across Canada. Do research on cost and availability if this is an approach that you wish to take.

Candidates often use a large van parked in a farmer's field, or a large A-frame truck-mounted sign, or passenger vehicles that have decals or even painted to deliver a candidate or party message. Some candidates will have a name on a large tractor-trailer unit parked in a field near their jurisdiction. These are all effective techniques if permitted in your area.

While some of these may not be consistent with a local ordinance or bylaw, most of the time candidates seek the tools that they can afford and attempt to be unique in message delivery or name recognition tools that are used for the four weeks just prior to an election. There are, of course, various exceptions to all these assumptions depending on the order of government and legislation governing campaign-related matters.

For campaigns that require workers who must interface with the public such as when door knocking or participating at some forums, wearing a name tag is important and at times required. If name tags are required or part of an election campaign, the name of the candidate and the name of the worker must appear in large print, be clearly visible and be placed high on the outermost garment. And of course, branding and colouring again should be a strong consideration for such paraphernalia.

Other ideas that candidates have chosen to use are restaurant place mats or communicating or advertising on small, public newsletters that might be out and about in a community.

For supporter badges, there are kits that can be purchased to make such badges quite inexpensively. Badges can also be made by specialty shops that manufacture them. This is also another opportunity for a gift in kind if you can find a business that is prepared to manufacture some badges for a candidate or their team.

Often you may observe a candidate standing near busy traffic locations, waving, or you may see a team of supporters waving a candidate's sign near a busy roadway. While it is difficult to imagine that someone will not vote for you because of that tactic, it is perhaps effective because, after all, that approach is about gaining candidate name recognition.

One more small tip is that you should use the word "vote," not "elect." In other words, on signs or in advertisements, state "Vote Susan Jones," not "Elect Susan Jones." This so election signs can be re-used if the candidate runs for re-election.

Getting your name and the message out in every way possible, in every way that you can afford or have resources to do, will maximize the probability of receiving a vote.

CHAPTER 8
DOOR KNOCKING

8.1 IMPACT AND PREPARATION

THE IMPACT OF DOOR KNOCKING IS REMARKABLE, and my experiences are nothing but positive and motivating. You may recall from earlier chapters that research has shown that there are three overarching important elements: first is organization structure, second is quality canvassing and the third is door knocking efficiency.

I believe that Laurie Hahn, MP for a federal riding in Edmonton door knocked his constituency several times, alone and with teams over a two-election cycle with the intent of unseating the deputy prime minister at the time, and he eventually did so. He shared with me that he felt door knocking was the secret to his success. I believe he was correct.

In 2007, I chose to run for the mayor of the city that I live in. I was seeking the office against two competitors, one a relatively unknown candidate who had some significant businesspeople backing him, and the second a well-known previous mayor whose wife had served for nearly 20 years as well. I felt that I had to use every tactic known to electioneering at that time and use an approach that I felt would set me apart from my two competitors. I chose door knocking as my differentiator, and it helped in a remarkable way.

At that time, there were over 18,000 doors (mostly with doorbells) in St. Albert, Alberta and I set a goal to average 200 doors per day for 90 days and to become elected based on a strategy that was attempting to ask for one vote at a time. I did it all alone and wanted to do it alone.

Unlike many other tactics, door knocking is successful because it is about discussing issues and seeking support one vote and one person at a time. There is no substitute for it. It is motivating, refreshing and positive and has the added benefit of being filled with fresh air and exercise. This is at least the case in an urban setting where doors are close to each other and driving is not necessary, except to get to and from a particular neighbourhood each day.

During those 90 days, I knocked every day and into the evening and knocked for entire days many times. I had to start in the morning and some days I had to stop earlier than hoped, due to other engagement reasons. I was able to knock on all 18,842 doors during that time. That by itself was worthy of a press release, and I was able to garner attention and a newspaper story simply by the significance of it all. I was able to state, "Anyone who says I did not knock on their door is wrong. You may not have been home, but I was there." No one in the city of 50,000 disputed my claim, because no one could. I loved every minute of it.

It is said that door knocking is equal to one vote per house. While that statistic is certainly not able to be verified, it is a differentiator.

Earlier in the book I shared that friends and family may be worth 50 votes for each family member or close friend. When you knock on a friendly door, that door knock has the benefits of coming across some of the 1,000 people who you know or are related to. You can review many issues of common interest and appeal to those 1,000 to get out and vote (and to spread the word).

In door knocking, preparation matters.

Start by flossing your teeth.

With me daily was my vehicle in case I needed to stock up, rest or make notes. The vehicle had lawn signs in the back, spare pens, markers, spare door knocking cards, a change of clothing and supplies for all weather conditions. Do not leave wallets or purses in vehicles, and find ways to consolidate ID, cash or credit cards so that you are able to carry those items with you.

Figure 21. *Notice of door knocking location by long-time Mayor Stuart Houston in Spruce Grove, Alberta*

THE POLITICAL CAMPAIGN "HOW-TO" GUIDE

I carried about 150 door knocking cards while walking. Carrying more than that would cause my wrists to ache, because the cards were made of heavy material. I dressed in the same clothes every day and washed the same clothes every night. My shirt was the colour of my campaign materials. My name tag was large, visible just under my collar, with my name very large on it that said "Nolan Crouse, MAYOR Candidate." There was no mistaking my name nor what I was doing at the door.

My dress code was modest, light coloured and comfortable. My shoes were white runners and they started new. I wore no hat and the glasses I wore were not tinted. I had received the advice to wear non-tinted glasses so that people could see my eyes. I carried a pen between my fingers, the street map under my cards. Each night before heading out, my wife printed off for me the names of those who lived on the streets that I was heading toward. There was a reverse-lookup feature available with Telus phone pages at that time which would provide about 70% of the names for those living on any given street.

I also had a very small notepad to write down comments and if I had any follow-up from a house. Most of the time I did not, although every so often someone would ask for a lawn sign, an email from me for a reason, some follow-up if I got elected or other comments or requests that I had to record. I kept my tape recorder in the truck to record thoughts during my breaks. I began to track the common themes for post-election follow-up if I became elected. I had a highlighter felt-tip pen that would not leak into my pocket (use see-through red, bold enough to follow but not blacking out the addresses or street names). I used this pen to mark off the street that I just completed, so that I did not get confused, turned around or lost. I had to mark down where my vehicle was parked, because after two or three hours I would have to find my way back. My BlackBerry (not an iPhone then) was on silent and on vibrate. Candidates or volunteers should wear something with a loose pocket to keep key personal items securely held, such as ID and phones.

Also, in my truck were spare shoes, a rain poncho, granola bars, a thermos of fluids, a wet cloth, a comb, dental floss, lens cleaner materials, and sanitary wipes to wipe sweat or to keep my hands clean. If you are taking any medication, have that on your daily checklist.

If you are door knocking by driving from home to home in a rural setting, many of these above principles and checklists apply, but of course the time required going from one door to another changes depending on the area. Acreage areas are different than sprawling, rural areas and are different than a neighbourhood of single-family homes.

Figure 22. *Marked door knocking route map*

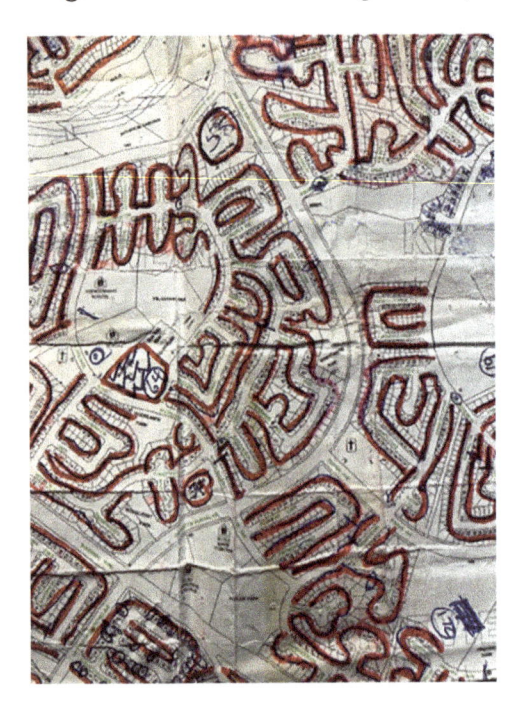

Also, during door knocking times, it may be fatiguing, may be during inclement weather, and other matters may get forgotten. While it may not seem important, even consider the small things such as when to gas up, having clothes pressed, when and how to pay your bills or do banking, or who is doing the laundry and what type of nutritional plan do you have that is energizing. Medication refills and other matters of personal importance need to be thought of weeks before the intense election campaign period. A campaign period is often very different for many people and the activities can become so laser-focused on door knocking or campaign activities, and other matters may arise such as new personal emergencies when least desired. All domestic and personal matters should be contemplated and pre-planned.

So, in summary, here is your supplies checklist for door knocking:

- Ballpoint pen
- Smartphone on vibrate only
- Non-tinted glasses (if you wear glasses)
- Comb
- Cash in pocket
- IDs in pocket

- Name tag
- Map
- Tylenol
- Door knocking cards
- Fluids to drink in thermoses
- Notebook
- Handheld tape recorder
- Energy or granola bars
- Watch
- Names of residents in the area
- Spare clothes
- Spare shoes
- Spare socks
- Rain poncho or umbrella
- Highlighter
- Medication
- Dental floss

8.2 IMAGE

Door knocking requires you to consider your image, and if you are going to have a team assist you in this regard, the team should also portray that same image. The image should always be a comfortable and casual dress code with no dresses, suits or ties. You are on someone's doorstep, driveway or front yard. Periodically, someone is near their vehicle or working on their yard or home exterior. They too are dressed to work, just like you or your volunteers. Portray the image of a worker, dressed to work for the voter and well-groomed. Most people know what is overdressed and what is underdressed or what it means to be dressed for the occasion. You need to be dressed for the occasion.

The colouring and name badge pinned on the clothes matter.

All volunteers must wear the same style of name tag, with their name and the name of the candidate in a font that anyone can read from a door knocking distance. The first glance of someone who answers the door will go from the knocker's face to the door knocker's name tag, and those glances will happen quickly.

An image of a smiling person, appropriately dressed, with a name tag on and well-groomed will almost always be respected, especially since you are on their turf. You are the visitor and they set the rules, but you set the tone.

For most doors visited, the candidate is not known to the person living behind that door. Therefore, the opening line needs to always be, "Hello, my name is Jane Doe, and I am here seeking the office of mayor in this community." After a brief pause by you, the next move is also yours, because that split-second pause will provide a verbal opportunity for the door opener. That first impression (you only get one chance to make that good first impression) is critical to the image, messaging and the next steps at that door. The rest is situational management based on how the conversation proceeds.

If no conversation is desired, a simple handout of the door knocking card is always provided along with a candidate thank you and a reminder about the election, and you part ways.

8.3 MAPS

Obtain from the riding, constituency, municipal office or band office a map of your community or boundaries of where your voters are located. You may have to purchase the map and they are likely inexpensive and worth it. Some county maps in Canada may even have the landowner's name on the maps, and that may assist with the door knocking if you have to drive from door to door in a rural setting.

Maps with addresses are important so that you know where you are or in case you need to have a campaign worker pick someone up on Election Day, deliver a lawn sign or a mail-in ballot. Keeping close track of where you are requires a map or a smartphone app/history and the discipline to note the information that is gathered or to be provided. Smartphone note-taking, texting yourself, tape recording or writing down notes are, of course, all dependent upon the preference of the campaign team and its leadership.

8.4 TEAM

You may choose to door knock with a team, and that is more often the case than going alone. Teamwork is fun, motivating and carries with it the ability to cover a lot of ground. I always suggest that the candidate must be in close proximity to the team, and while door knocking without the candidate is better than no door knocking at all, there is an element of added legitimacy if the candidate is with the team. If a resident says, "May I speak with the candidate?", you can share, "Yes, we will be right back with them," and then the volunteer can make it happen.

Equally important is that the candidate knocks with a planned script in mind. The script for all volunteers who are door knocking should be something like the following:

"Hello, my name is Jane Doe, and I am here campaigning for John Doe, who is also here in the neighbourhood if you wish to speak with him."

Again, teach your volunteers to exhibit that brief pause, and then the next move is also that of the volunteer. That split-second pause will provide an opening for the door opener to comment and demonstrate willingness or unwillingness to engage any further. That first impression (the volunteer is an extension of the candidate and also only gets one chance to make a good first impression on behalf of the candidate) is important to the image, the messaging and the next steps that occur at that door.

8.5 TACTICS

If the person answering the door is interested in engaging further, a next line for a candidate is also quite simple: "I would like to leave this small card with you, which has my contact information and a little about me (or the candidate) on it. If there is anything that you would like to speak about right now, I would love to chat." At that moment, the ball is moved quickly to the resident and most residents, because it is a cold call, will be very polite, caught off guard but perhaps even ready to engage if their mind is politically active. Most are not ready to engage at that very moment. There may be issues in that riding, there may be issues in the country, on the settlement, in the town or the region. The person may not even care about what office you are running for, because the important element at that time is simply to chat. Beyond that first few seconds of the engagement, conversations may go any number of ways, and the best candidates and volunteers are able to listen, speak in brief soundbites and bullet points, articulate elements of the platform with ease and demonstrate visually a willingness to listen by taking a note or two.

It is wise to record the name of that household if the conversation is in depth. It is wise to keep that data for future intelligence entry, and this is especially true if you are mining data for partisan purposes and future information purposes.

It is unwise to enter a home and never wise to sit down in a home unless there is clearly something so compelling that it is critical to the election success. It should be rare, however, in most campaigns to enter someone's home and sit.

If you are asked a question at the door, be sure you understand the question and use confirmation tools to assist you. Accents, language barriers, cultural use of words, poor listening, poor techniques by both participants (like in normal communications) may cause misunderstandings and frustration for the person asking the question.

If you are using the information provided about who may live in the home, you are also able to connect in your opening lines with "hello, my name is Jane Doe, and I am here seeking the office of councillor in this community. Are you Mr. Jones?" Remember to introduce yourself first, because you are on their turf and it may cause uneasiness if you come across like you know the residents before they know who you are.

In almost 100% of the cases, the handout that you offer will be accepted by the individual answering the door. If you hold the handout in front of you in a polite and non-intrusive way, it can be used as the bridge. The eye contact of the person answering the door can move from the eyes to the badge, back to the faces and to the door knocking card, all within a matter of a second. Comfort is established as the person at the door is able to say "thank you, no thank you" or engage in conversation.

Teaching your campaign team this entire approach and using some role playing will assist in the interaction to be fun, engaging and non-confrontational. There are very few who engage in negative or confrontational conversation unless there is something that is very volatile or is fresh on a voter's mind at the time the doorbell rings. This can be the case with partisan door knocking especially.

If there is no one home, cardstock election door drops may easily be slid into the doorjamb if there is no screen door or mailbox. Do not attempt to open any screen door or exterior door under any circumstances. It is inappropriate 100% of the time and reasons do not need to be explained. The cardstock should be 14 or 16 pt. paper as described earlier in the book.

If there is no easy door slot or no mailbox, the door knocking card can be tucked 20% under a door mat. That will ensure it is not blown away, and if it is brightly coloured it will eventually be seen by the residents.

If there is a lot of mail already in the mailbox, slide the card in so that it is protruding, highly visible and sticking out on top of all other mail or fliers in the box. You will need to assess the highest traffic house-entry door and go to that door first.

If there is a sign that says No Fliers, it is up to the candidate if they see their card as a flier or not. I suggest that you leave a card at every door regardless of what the condition was of the front door, the mailbox or the steps, etc. I do not judge by whom and how it may be seen or picked up or discarded. A candidate's job is to seek support to become elected, and it is wise to demonstrate your democratic right to seek votes in a variety of ways. Deciding whether a "no fliers" sign meant no door knocking cards is a choice any candidate may wish to make differently. I always left a card.

Do not knock on any door before 9:30 a.m. under any circumstances. There are many reasons, including shift workers just falling asleep, people eating breakfast, late morning risers and also the fact that the clothes worn by the person who is answering the door at that time are often not the clothes they wish to be seen in. School-aged children getting ready for school, adults getting ready for work and many other morning activities occur before 9:30 a.m., and courtesy prevails.

Do not knock on any door after 8:30 p.m. because of bedtime for children, and it seems to be the time of the day when people start shutting down in many aspects. Personal safety at night is also a factor for candidates and volunteers.

The time of day when the highest percentage of people are home is at about 6:00 p.m.; however, it is also the time of the day when people are the most agitated with a doorbell ringing. Dinner time, children's activities, after work activities, conversation time of parents and their children and conversation time of spouses appear to be the main reasons for this being such a challenging timeframe.

Do not knock before 10:00 a.m. on a Sunday morning under any circumstances.

There are likely dogs in about 40% of households, and it is critical that as a door knocker you protect yourself from lunging animals. A technique to employ is to ring the doorbell or knock but always step back half a metre for various reasons, not the least of which is to give the homeowner time to control an escaping cat, barking dog or lunging dog. Always believing a dog is at the door is a wise practice, because 40% of the time it will be the case – and a small percentage of those times, the dog may not be friendly. Never reach to an animal to find out either. An attentive ear when attending a door usually provides a clue of whether anyone or a dog is home.

If no one is home or no one answers the door, write a polite note on the door knocking card in your own handwriting that says, "Sorry I missed you," followed by your signature. I would pre-sign about 200 of these and have them with me in my hip pocket if I needed to use a pre-signed one. Therefore, if you needed to use a signed one, a swift swipe into a hip pocket allows you to grab a card and move quickly to the next door after leaving the signed card behind.

After ringing a doorbell or knocking, there may be a moment of silence that can be telling, such as a sound in the house of someone running, shuffling of a chair, or other noises that may give away whether someone is coming to the door, running to hide or leaving out a back door. Each noise is a signal to pay attention to and should be honoured. Minors who are home alone may not be permitted to answer a door, and that is only one example of reasons why there may be noise followed by silence, and it occurs often.

While it is not an easy decision for a door knocker with respect to door knocking, a child answering the door who appears to be between the ages of 10 and 15 is at an awkward stage in their lives where they may not be permitted to engage in a conversation with a strange adult and may even be told by their parents to be dishonest at the door if you ask, "Is an adult home?" As such, unless the child appears under the age of 10, when it is likely there is an adult in the dwelling, my advice is not to put a minor in the uncomfortable position of having to not tell the truth. They may not wish to accommodate you as a stranger at the door. Provide the card and ask that it be left on the kitchen counter, and simply move on to the next house. Youth may share that their parents are in bed, in the shower or in the backyard to indicate that an adult is nearby, when indeed the youth may be home alone. A real young child, however, is more than happy to turn the door over to an adult.

It can be common for two or three people to door knock together as those who are running for the same order of office such as councillors running for office in a city. This allows a lot of ground to be covered door knocking for each other and with each other (seen by some as a slate when done with two or more candidates). Delivering door knocking cards and door knocking in a zigzag fashion or alternating houses makes for good teamwork and optimizes many factors. Having appropriate lines of communication to connect with the other candidate(s) who are with you also enhances such an approach to door knocking.

If you are door knocking as part of a campaign team, the team needs to have its lines rehearsed, because the team cannot speak fully for the candidate but certainly can speak the party line more easily. The platform of a federal, territorial or provincial party can reasonably be shared at the door by team members, but when it comes to a candidate's view, the words used by the door knocking volunteer need to be crystal clear. Some people remember what is stated and are willing to challenge anyone who appears to not be sharing appropriate information.

8.6 PACE

Pace of door knocking depends on the number of door knockers, and while the data below in Figure 23 does not hold true for all candidates or all campaigns, the information below can be extrapolated using a linear approach to get some sense of the amount of time that is required in a true urban setting to cover areas.

Pace is quicker in the daytime and slower at dinner time for numerous reasons, including darkness and the fact that a higher percentage of individuals are home in evenings.

Pace is quicker on weekdays than on weekends, when residents take more time to discuss issues. There is a higher number of people in a household able to answer a door on Saturdays and Sundays.

Pace is slower on Sundays between 10:00 a.m. and 8:00 p.m., when it appears more people are willing to take time to engage with candidates – plus there is a higher percentage of residents who are home on Sundays.

Permission must be obtained from apartment building management or condo development ownership/management when the site is gated or when a building's main doors are locked, as a matter of practice and policy. Pace is brisk once approval is obtained and once the association permits the candidate to enter a complex.

Generally, in urban door knocking, it may be tempting to travel at maximum pace by taking shortcuts across lawns or yards or other private property areas to get from door to door quickly. The sidewalks and driveways are the only paths recommended. Getting caught shortcutting will be embarrassing and is simply wrong to do.

Figure 23. *Tracking of door knocking (partial spreadsheet)*

Total Km Planned:	737	Total Km Remaining =	595

Total Door knocking minutes done	4,340
Doors per minute done	0.835

Door Knocking Tracking

Date	Days Left to Vote	Where Did I knock?	Door Knocking Minutes	Total Door Bells Rung	Min. Help With Me	Women	Men	Total Men+ Wom.	% Home	Time of Day	Estimate of Km Covered	Day of the Week
Totals to date			3,645	3,625	695	726	567	1,293	35.67		142	
21-Jun	116	North Ridge	270	235	0	39	24	63	27	Daytime	9.19	Thurs
22-Jun	115	North Ridge	175	160	0	32	19	51	32	Daytime	6.26	Fri
23-Jun	114	North Ridge	265	230	0	54	54	108	47	Daytime	8.99	Sat
24-Jun	113	Deer Ridge	270	210	0	57	55	112	53	Afternoon	8.21	Sun
25-Jun	112	Deer Ridge	290	255	0	48	32	80	31	Daytime	9.97	Mon
26-Jun	111	Deer Ridge	65	77	0	11	8	19	25	Afternoon	3.01	Tue
27-Jun	110	Deer Ridge	300	269	60	52	33	85	32	Daytime	10.52	Wed
28-Jun	109	Deer Ridge	165	214	65	51	27	78	36	Daytime	8.37	Thurs
29-Jun	108	Deer Ridge	395	316	0	72	53	125	40	Daytime	12.36	Fri
30-Jun	107	Heritage Lakes	330	331	90	72	61	133	40	Daytime	12.94	Sat
01-Jul	106	Heritage Lakes	215	287	135	55	45	100	35	Afternoon	11.22	Sun
02-Jul	105	Heritage Lakes	310	392	140	85	77	162	41	Daytime	15.33	Mon
03-Jul	104	Heritage Lakes	290	241	0	37	37	74	31	Daytime	9.42	Tue
04-Jul	103	Heritage Lakes	305	408	205	61	42	103	25	Daytime	15.95	Wed

8.7 DATA COLLECTION

The data below is from urban door knocking during a municipal campaign.

The data collected was as follows:

Doors knocked on	18,842
Doors knocked per minute	0.786
Total kilometres walked	737

Percent of someone answering the door	37.54%
Percent of women answering	58%
Percent of men answering	42%
Percent of children answering	<1%

Keeping this data may allow you to prepare somewhat, although the data shows nothing highly compelling to influence the strategy significantly, other than perhaps serving as a benchmark for how you plan your time.

8.8 TRACKING

During the election campaign or at the end of an election campaign, all data gathered and intelligence obtained will be helpful for a candidate to follow-up on and record for future campaigns.

There may be several themes of important door knocking input that can allow a candidate to become more effective at helping to govern in a jurisdiction if elected.

Of course, promising to do something about issues raised at various doors is unwise, but promising to represent, to listen and to perhaps respond is a wise approach. The choice of words, while perhaps not always said and heard the same by everyone at a door, is important. The principle that you as a candidate should employ at the door is to be careful what you say and be *more* careful about what you promise. People will remember.

Below is an example of how the data may be displayed when your door knocking feedback is tabulated.

Figure 24. *Door knocking data summary (partial actual spreadsheet)*

	Door knocking feedback topics / Issue	Mentions	Comments / Comments as Appropriate
1	Taxes	128	Education tax
2	Recreation Centre	72	
3	Basic Services (Fundamentals)	59	grass, paths, older areas
4	West Regional Road	43	Cost, Schedule, Province
5	Recycling + blue bag + Curbside	40	big stuff, plastics
6	Regional cooperation	23	
7	Business friendly + Economic Develop.	23	80-20
8	Seniors	22	Bus passes
9	Transit	17	empty busses, Saturdays, amalgamation
10	Affordable Housing	17	
11	Sidewalk repairs	13	
12	Grandin Mall issues	12	Height, tree barrier, yes, 13 OK, too high
13	Condominium split mill rate	12	
14	Waste/Garbage/Tags	11	User Pay
15	Bylaw enforcement (speeding)	11	dogs
16	Tree Maintenance	10	Fruit, dead, pruning
17	Vandalism	9	

8.9 DOOR KNOCKING STORIES

While there are many stories about door knocking that I could tell from my four campaigns, I share a few below.

STORY # 1

One election (my first election) was on a Monday, and I was door knocking on the preceding Thursday and my BlackBerry vibrated in my pocket. I was between houses on a street. I answered the call, and it was the agent that I had hired to assist me in landing a coaching job with the Chinese men's national ice hockey team. He was calling to confirm that I was being offered the coaching job in Harbin, China as co-coach to help the men's team advance up the world rankings. My heart raced as he was not aware that parallel to me seeking a professional coaching job in China, I was also seeking to run for political office locally. I was unsure of my chances of being offered the job to coach in China, so this elected official role was a backup plan in some respects. I collected the details, thanked him, of course, and said that I would call him the following week. Since I was elected on that subsequent Monday, one of the first phone calls on the Tuesday was to the agent who negotiated my job, to let him know that I was hanging up the skates. Yogi Berra said, "When you get to a Y in the road, take it," and this was one of my Y's in my lifelong road.

STORY # 2

One time I rang a doorbell and spoke with a young girl of about 10 years of age. After introducing myself, I quickly asked her to pass on the door knocking card to an adult in the home. She did not give me a comfortable answer but took the door knocking card, and I moved on to the next home. About 10 minutes later, as I was crossing the street, she ran up behind me and handed me back the card and said, "You can have this back, my parents don't believe in democracy." It is a lesson that we simply do not know the circumstances at any door, and therefore, one cannot prejudge anything when door knocking.

STORY # 3

My paternal grandmother (Laura Crouse) died in 1936, and other than my father and his siblings, I did not know anyone who had ever met her. I knocked on a door one time and a very elderly woman answered, and surprisingly, she had right in her home a lawn sign of mine that I had not left there. She told me she had stolen it, because it provided her a childhood memory. She asked me if my grandmother was a travelling saleswoman in the 1920s, and I told her "yes." She said, "I knew your grandmother and actually slept in the same bed as her once in the '20s." She shared that my grandmother had come by her farm place in a blizzard and her family gave my grandmother a bed for the night so that she did not have to travel at night in her horse and buggy. She said, "Your grandma slept with me in my bed. Your grandma was well known and we trusted her, but I have never forgotten her name, and when I saw your last name I thought of her." This 90+ old woman telling me this story in 2007 about my very own grandmother who had died 70 years earlier was surreal. I was thrilled she stole one of my signs, and I clearly did not want it put back wherever she took it from.

STORY # 4

One time when I was knocking on doors, I ran across the same person twice at different doors at different houses the same day. I was taken aback. As it turns out, it happened many times while door knocking as people house-sit, live in two homes, babysit, visit relatives and more. When it occurs, it is a great conversation opportunity both for the door knocker or the person answering the door. The time that I knocked on the over 18,000 doors, I came across the same person seven different times whom I had seen at a different house previously.

STORY # 5

As a two-time incumbent, I door knocked on one door and the woman who answered the door knew a lot more about me than I thought seemed normal, and it even caused me some alarm. After learning more about how she knew so much about me, she also told me that she was stalking me. I reported it to the police, and they reported back to me that they subsequently visited her. As it turns out, she was having some mental health challenges and there was nothing more they could or should do. I left it alone, but to this day I remember where she lives and it always was in the back of my mind, wondering what her motives or plans were to get to know so much about my personal life and work schedule.

STORY # 6

I knocked on a door and a woman answered who was homeschooling her seven children, and everyone came to the door. It took some time to address many questions, but later the woman who answered became one of my election volunteers, delivered fliers and years later ran in both a school board and a federal election herself. I had motivated her to serve, and her children and I talked many times over the years as they grew up.

STORY # 7

At one door I knocked on, the woman who answered the door opened it widely so that I could see what she had posted on the wall in eye view of all door knocking candidates. It was a flip chart with the important issues listed taped onto the house entrance wall. On the flip chart was a list of the important issues to her, and she proceeded to question me on the list. I was not sure if I passed her test, but certainly, she was engaged in the campaign.

STORY # 8

Similarly, I knocked on a door and the woman who answered had a list of all candidates on the wall inside the door and she was checking off who had been to her door during that campaign. She told me that she was going to vote for only those who came to her door, and as I spoke with her, she shared that there were six openings for local councillors available and she only voted for door knockers. She put a felt pen check mark beside my name as I stood there.

STORY # 9

I approached a home which had a sunflower seed stuck in the doorbell, and before I hit the doorbell, I had to determine what to do or what approach to take. I pushed the doorbell gently, although the glass cover on it was broken. When the couple answered the door, they shared that they kept a sunflower seed stuck in the doorbell and it attracted birds. When a bird would peck at the sunflower seed, at times the doorbell would ring, and they would get a view of the bird. They shared that a blue jay was the most prolific at ringing that bell, and in fact, one bird actually had gotten electrocuted at that doorbell. The couple took me into their backyard, which was forested with the intent of attracting birds, and the yard certainly had attracted many who were there to feed and nest. It was an urban bird sanctuary.

Door knocking matters.

CHAPTER 9
THE COVID LESSONS

9.1 THE GAME CHANGED FOREVER

THE COVID-19 PANDEMIC MAY HAVE CHANGED CAMPAIGN strategies forever, and the impact of social media was made more important, and perhaps forever more important, than before the pandemic.

Finding approaches to increase followers on various social media outlets has become increasingly important, and the pandemic has made these platforms critically important for campaigning and messaging between elections. There is no question that incumbents who work at growing followers and friends using the numerous approaches have advantages over non-incumbents. It is equally true that those seeking office for the first time must find new and unique ways to grow followers throughout the preceding years to assist in name recognition, and ultimately in campaigning when they choose to seek office.

Networking organizations, befriending others, blogs, videos and YouTube channels are just a few examples of approaches.

Grow your network earlier rather than later if you have any desire to run for office someday.

9.2 DOOR KNOCKING

Door knocking in British Columbia during the pandemic was completed by many individuals during the non-lockdown times of the 2020 pandemic, yet with a specific strategy.

The door knocking strategy during the pandemic began with the door knocking person leaving a door drop brochure at a door, then knocking with plastic gloves on (or ringing a bell). The door knocker then moved a further distance from the door (two to three metres) with a significantly upsized name tag. This seemed to be an acceptable approach to those who answered doors. Upon answering a door, the door knocker would proceed to advise the person answering the door as follows:

"Hello, my name is Bob Jones. I am seeking your support in the upcoming British Columbia provincial election and I have left a little card about me in your mailbox."

That line allows for the linkage from the door knocker (candidate or representative) to the person answering the door and to the door drop card and lowers the fear of the spreading of the virus.

Door knocking still matters; demonstrating work ethic and commitment remains possible and required.

As Nike says, "Just do it."

9.3 MAIL-IN BALLOTS

This is an emerging, newer approach to increasing the probability and ease for someone voting. If you have access to the tools and are able to make this approach easier, find a way to do so. Communicating the approach as a candidate and assisting others in making it happen will increase the probability that someone will vote for you. Be known as a candidate who wishes to make voting approaches easier for the voter.

The mail-in ballot is one pandemic impact that needs to now form part of a candidate's campaign strategy whether there is an election in the midst of a pandemic or not. Pandemic or no pandemic, this approach will likely grow in its use.

Help make it happen.

9.4 ADVANCED VOTING

Advanced voting, like mail-in voting and ultimately online voting, will likely grow over time. Caring candidates will help make it easy by communicating when and where one can advance vote. Encourage organizers and decision makers to increase the ease, timeframe and opportunities. As a candidate, it is advised that you support all aspects of voters being able to vote, including advanced voting and ballot submission options. The same could be said for mobile unit voting the days leading up to and on election days. These approaches may very well increase in the years ahead, and candidates need to adjust accordingly. Changes in election approaches and how voters make a determination who to vote for reinforces even more the importance of door knocking and social media linkages.

COVID-19 has hastened the approaches to alternate methods of voting, and it is wise to be known as a candidate who approves any and all aspects of voting, any time of day or night, at any location and by any secure means.

9.5 VIRTUAL MEETINGS

Facebook live is one of many examples where virtual meetings may occur. Zoom, Webex, Google Meet, Microsoft Teams and other online platforms are all great examples that should be used. These approaches were used in British Columbia and may be used more into the future across Canada. Facebook and other related meeting forums can also be utilized after door knocking hours end. Catching the late-night viewer or someone who likes to be online later in an evening can work independent of a pandemic, but the pandemic increased the number of activities that used virtual campaigning in BC.

Many outdoor events with proper distancing were also planned, supplementing these virtual meetings.

9.6 ELECTRONIC VOTING

Electronic voting will continue to grow over time. If it is easy and secure, it is advised that you develop a separate strategy to drive voters to their online voting option. This is an emerging approach that will take foothold in 2022 and beyond in Canada.

Like advanced and mail-in voting, be known as the candidate that approves of any and all aspects of voting, any time of day or night, at any location and by any means.

CHAPTER 10
DETAILS GET YOU TO ELECTION DAY

10.1 THE TO-DO LIST

THROUGHOUT THIS BOOK ARE MANY TO-DOS THAT will assist you in planning some of your details. While it is not possible to capture every detail in every election, it is hoped that the listings within the chapters plus the information in the appendix will trigger thoughts or be helpful as you embark on a potential role of elected service.

10.2 THE NAYSAYERS

Most of what has been covered in this book are the things to do, the possibilities, the actions and the philosophies regarding election campaigning. I have not covered the intense obligation that service to others is intended to be for elected officials. That is a book unto itself and indeed has been written about by many.

What I have not spoken of are those who are willing and able to set you back, those who do not agree with you or those who are intent on ensuring your election or re-election is unsuccessful or damaged in some way. I will touch briefly on that matter here, although not exhaustively for there are many aspects to this topic that are best covered elsewhere.

You will encounter those who politely disagree with you, while others will vehemently disagree with you. In party politics or for incumbents, this is especially the case. In non-partisan contests, there is much more civil discourse than in partisanship where the emotions run higher. There is also usually less concern with those entering an election contest for the first time, because often the public is prepared to give someone a pass or may not know a newbie well enough to know if they should be supported or not. Incumbents face more naysayers and opposition than non-incumbents. Some people simply dislike government and/or politicians.

That said, you do need to pay some attention to what is being said. The feedback you receive from the naysayers (or those who clearly oppose you) needs to be understood in context. Negative comments coming from an opposition member attempting to seek the same seat as you are less concerning than negative comments coming from people you know or if there is already pent-up anger toward a platform position you take. There may be social media trolls who are simply attempting to disrupt your flow, harm the spirit of your volunteers or plant self-doubt in your own abilities and positions on issues. I believe that while you cannot be overly distracted by this information, you simply need to be willing to change tactics if you have to, be willing to disagree professionally and take the time to spend only the time it deserves to correct the record or address a matter of misinformation. You and your team will not have time to respond to every social media post that takes you away from other, perhaps more important elements of your campaign.

My advice is as follows:

1. Understand the source of the naysayers if possible.
2. Understand the context of the disagreement or hostility.
3. Understand the issue or the questions being raised; there may be valuable insight to learn from.
4. Address the source(s) professionally and when you have time to do so.
5. Always tell the truth, set the record straight and address others by Mr., Ms. or M. when you do not know their name.
6. A candidate cannot take time away from door knocking to address all naysayers.
7. If possible, address the online forums by communicating late at night or early in the morning.
8. If someone is managing your communication and/or social media accounts, continue to tell the truth and stick with facts.
9. At the door, do not argue, and in fact look down at that friendly notebook you are carrying and simply make notes.
10. When in crowds, at group gatherings or at open microphone forums, stay calm, speak in soundbites and do not argue.
11. Always thank everyone for their opinion or question; this may disarm or quell emotions on a topic.
12. Keep your emotions in check.
13. If the naysayer is overly harmful to your psyche, your volunteers or your family, it is acceptable to not engage.

10.3 TREATMENT OF OTHER CANDIDATES

Treat all candidates like you wish to be treated at all times. While there may be a strategy that you employ or that your team employs, spoken about in an earlier chapter (do you go high or go low), the general rule of thumb is to treat other candidates well. Some of their supporters may actually be undecided voters. Perhaps their family actually does not wish them to win a seat and some voters may be judging your behaviour and conduct and may use your treatment of others as a key point in how they decide who to vote for.

You may also serve on the same governing body with your opposition after the election or after a future election, and bad blood may carry over.

As difficult as it may be from time to time, biting your tongue in some situations, rising above the fray or turning a blind eye to matters of disagreement or discontent is usually the best policy during a contest, unless someone wishes to attack your integrity or your family, in which case you may need to confront it. Confrontations can also be professional and measured, and it is always wise to behave with tact.

Finally, as shared in earlier chapters, consider teaming up with other candidates for the Election Day and post-election day activities. This can include sharing celebration venues, sharing food and volunteers teaming up on Election Day or post-election day office cleanup or street cleanup. Teaming up and combining resources can make things happen quickly. The benefits of working well with others will trickle into the volunteer corps, and indeed it will also show at the ballot box. People working with people may result in increased voter turnout or increased support for you as a candidate. A rising tide lifts all ships.

Finally, treatment of others should not need to be a list of to-dos and a list of not-to-dos but should be a behavioural trait displayed because it is a value you hold. For most, the treatment of others is usually most evident in their character that is demonstrated when under pressure.

10.4 TREATMENT OF NON-VOTERS

Much interaction will occur with non-eligible non-voters. This group may be non-eligible for many reasons. They may be a group of minors or school-aged children who are seeking to learn about politics. These people may be short-term renters, recent immigrants or others who may not be eligible to vote. This interaction matters significantly, because these people may influence others who do vote.

Some schools actually will study candidates and platforms and elections as part of the curriculum, and what better time to study that topic than during an election period? For this reason, attending school events should be encouraged, attending immigrant gatherings and more are opportunities to interact with others. As always, one cannot judge who influences whom during an election period. A simple illustration is that grade six students studying candidates as part of a curriculum will likely discuss their studies with their parents, which is an opportunity for children to influence their parents.

During one election campaign, one of my competitors decided not to return emails from grade six students who were doing a candidate assessment by studying the various candidates. I answered all the emails from the same students, and he answered none. He stated, "Grade six students don't vote." He was correct. I answered these emails just before bed every night during the campaign period and I will never know if it helped, but I was elected and he was not.

Non-voters are married to voters, non-voters live with voters, non-voters are sons and daughters of voters, are neighbours of voters, work with voters and more. Non-voters are volunteers, lawn sign hosts and donors. Non-voters matter, and it is plain and simple.

10.5 YOU JUST DON'T KNOW WHO...

Throughout this book I have shared a few times that we just don't know who influences whom in an election, and I wish to state it again. Just like my comment in the previous section, the influence is beyond what we can imagine.

A co-worker of mine from 20 years prior to one of my election campaigns had moved to a different city, and he actually sent a letter to the editor of the local newspaper outlining my character and strengths. It is those kinds of occurrences when you realize that you do not know where the support or influence may come from. A previous co-worker, a coached player or an acquaintance are all sources of influence on others. Political influence when it comes to influencing the voters is about spreading the word to a maximum number of people about a candidate in hopes the voter first chooses to vote, and second, chooses to vote for that candidate. Good reports about any candidate spread to others as well as bad reports spread to others.

Every election, I got asked (especially as an incumbent and especially as a mayor) by many, while door knocking or on the street, "Who else should I vote for?" The rule of thumb for an incumbent is to avoid being too prescriptive with this answer, because the person asking may know more about other candidates than you know they know. They may be testing you, and they may be seeking inside information. They may spread the word to others about what you shared, and that may become problematic.

My advice on that question is to say something like, "I can work with anyone and may have to work with anyone. Yes, I think I can work easily with John Doe, but I can work with anyone that you choose to vote for." While I tipped my hat periodically in a very coy approach, I was cautious and calculated with that answer always.

Derogatory comments about others will invariably find their way back to the candidate being spoken about, because that is the way the word is spread, especially during election campaigns when the stakes are higher and word-spreading is the name of the game.

Penny Reeves, that well-respected councillor I spoke about earlier in the book, shared with me her advice about how to behave during an election campaign and subsequently as an elected official once elected to office. She shared, "Make no derogatory comments ever about anyone." Separately, a lawyer and a councillor, Doug Ritzen, said something similar to me when he shared with me, "Wounds won't heal."

10.6 JUST WHEN YOU THOUGHT YOU HAD IT ALL FIGURED OUT

There may be something that comes to light in the midst of a campaign, something that is important to capitalize on or address, or breaking news and time may be of the essence to address it. If you are alone door knocking or locked away preparing for a speech, continue to check emails, social media and texts every 30 minutes for matters that may be emergent. You may not be able to address every message immediately but addressing something emerging requires a candidate to be nimble enough to do so.

There is no rule book for how to handle any emerging issue or crisis. The crisis may involve you or it may involve the party or a competitor. In the book *Crisis Management* by Steven Fink (given to me by a friend in 1987 during a work crisis of mine), Fink emphasizes that in every crisis there is one constant, and that is that the person at the "head" of the organization in crisis must be the person that is to communicate to those needing to hear more. At times we see leaders, political candidates and others disappear during difficult times, awaiting a more opportune time to address an issue. Getting the facts out and getting in front of any crisis in the midst of a campaign is critical.

While a matter may not be a crisis, there will be curve balls thrown that need to be addressed. It may be a volunteer resigning, a winter storm causing havoc with signs, or a personal matter that cannot wait. In one four-week campaign, I saw one candidate having to take two weeks off due to a death in the family, and who, for religious and family reasons was totally unavailable. The campaign did not recover, and the candidate was not elected, even while the volunteers admirably performed the duties they had agreed to perform.

So, be in touch with others and be willing and able to rally others for change. Handle things in stride, as life deals us these cards regularly and campaign times are no exception. Indeed, there may be matters such as a lack of money, inadequate or unqualified personnel leading a part of the campaign, scandals (real or perceived) or emerging new significant electorate issues at the top of the list. These can become surprises during campaign periods.

As the saying goes, "Just when you thought you had the perfect mousetrap invented, along come bigger mice."

10.7 THE DAYS (MONTHS) BEFORE YOU ARE OFFICIALLY A CANDIDATE

If you are contemplating running for office at some time in your life, it is never too late to set yourself up to do so. Demonstrating a desire to join the public service as an elected official may come to you quickly, like it did with me one year. Often, however, many contemplate such a notion for months or even years. If it is on your mind, think about how you are able to learn about the organization, the community, the party, governance or other related matters that you will need to know about to run a campaign or become elected. If you have significant interest in federal elections, consider joining a federal campaign team or a board of directors of a riding. Consider donating or attending conventions and becoming connected with those who may be mentors or role models.

The same goes provincially for political parties or candidates. Volunteer for campaigns or at rallies. Join boards that are commensurate with learning more about the party, the approach and the entire culture of the area of interest. Similarly, if you wish to run for a school board or a town or county council, consider volunteering to serve on civic committees that may need your expertise or time. Consider serving on a library board or other boards to get an insight into governance within your community.

Consider reading books on the subject, researching online or attending courses that cater to such skill development. Perhaps you need speaking skills and you may be wise to join a Toastmasters club, as an example.

So, unless you have an epiphany or are tapped on the shoulder at the last minute prior to an election (also quite common), setting yourself up to have some insight into what you might be getting involved in clearly has advantages. Of course, equally important is the network of contacts and supporters that you find yourself around who may be willing to assist you in any number of ways in the event you choose to seek office.

The sooner you set yourself up for success, the higher the probability that success will come your way in this regard. The world starves for leaders, and this perhaps is your category of leading.

10.8 THE DAY OF AND DAY AFTER BECOMING AN OFFICIAL CANDIDATE

Once you are nominated or once the legal processes are passed whereby all paperwork, forms, funds and signatures are in place, the work changes from preparing to campaign to actually campaigning. While this timeframe varies depending upon a number of factors, this gap is about four weeks in most situations across Canada and with most orders of government.

Checking out such timelines and milestones are critically important, because at times the window for submission of information may be tight and may even require that you attend or submit paperwork in person. All these details matter, and the day after you are an official candidate, you can begin officially and legally campaigning using the plan that you have put in place.

Generally, although not always required, the current governing body that you are seeking to serve on will continue to be the governing body (or individuals such as a mayor or reeve) in charge and will still technically remain in charge. A dissolution may occur of most of the work, the roles and responsibilities, but in case there is an emergent matter, the incumbent may still need to act accordingly as the governing person or group. The formal election process will often occur through a legal command being made by the appropriate authority (such as the writ being dropped).

Before the campaign period begins, pre-purchase any gifts that you plan on giving out after the election. Your spouse, family or campaign manager may receive something more than simply a thank-you card! Think about every detail so that it is not forgotten or so that you are able to fully dedicate yourself to the new role if you are successful in being elected.

After the election, issue a press release and send out the thanks that you had contemplated. Remember that spreadsheet with all the contacts? This is one time to use it.

Figure 25. *Volunteer list*

	Name (last)	Name (first)	#	Street Address	Phone #	email	Thanks sent	Other
				Volunteer List				
1	Anderson	Jan	33	Rayond Street	555-444-2222	Jan@jananderson.com	Yes	Helped with signs
2	Babiuk	Jill	45	Super Road	555-444-2229	Jil@jillwebsite.com	No	Was a lawn sign host
3	Chinook	Robert	6	Area Red	555-444-2345	Bchinook@chinook.ca	No	Treasurer
4	Doots	Dick	7	Subway Drive	555-444-4567	dick@doots.ca	No	Campaign Manager
5	Everson	James	9	Axel Street	555-444-9999	everson@jamese.ca	No	Brochure drop
6	Fairmont	Fred	8	Ham Crescent	555-444-2221	fredfair@fredfair.com	No	Door knocking help
7								
8								
9								
10								
11								
12								
13								
14								
15								
16								

Let the press know where you will be on the night of the election and provide them your contact information.

Once you are an official candidate, "game on," as is said by many.

10.9 ELECTION DAY

It's showtime.

You are still one vote behind the leader. You have one more call to make. You have one more door to knock on. This is the longest day of the campaign. This is the day you ensure you are ready for Election Day, because it is Election Day.

Are your volunteers in place driving shut-ins to the voting station? Is your email inbox empty? Is all your door knocking complete? If not, knock on a few more. Based on where you might be the most successful in an area, region or subregion of a constituency or community, given that you do not have many hours left, choose to perform your last campaigning efforts in the area that has the highest potential for voters to vote for you. This improves the probability of you picking up those last two votes to catapult you past the leader.

While it is wise to drive around in the early mornings and late nights often during an election campaign, on the day before and day of the election it is critical to ensure someone is checking the street signs to see if they are standing and not windblown or vandalized.

This is the day that you have the highest degree of expectations of your volunteers to ensure they are performing all their Election Day activities. Be kind and considerate, and yet also be demanding and appealing to others. Fatigue and rest are for later.

Yogi Berra said, "It gets late early." Yes, it sure does in elections.

This is the day whereby you rally everyone to vote. This is the final communication day, a full day of emails and texting and phoning to appeal to anyone and everyone who is available to vote to get out and vote. This is when you are tweeting and posting on Instagram and Facebook posts are rapid pace all day long. One last professional LinkedIn post is important.

Tag as many as you can and are able to who are within your voting community, appealing for their vote. This is the time when you cannot be shy or humble. This is the day for action.

Ensure your street signs are all standing; people need to see an image that is unstoppable.

The phone lines are busy, the text lines are busy and the drivers getting those who need a ride are busy.

Every communication mechanism that is permitted with legislation is employed today.

Vote for yourself and only yourself when you have a ballot that is seeking voting for multiple candidates such as a councillor, where you may have multiple choices. Suggest to your closest of friends and family to do the same, making them alert to the fact that a vote for someone other than you is negating the vote for you. This is easy to understand, but not intuitively natural for most to think this way. For example, the data shows that historically, if there are more than three running for three openings on a ballot, that the average number of votes cast is about 2.5 out of 3.0. This means not everyone votes for three candidates if there are three openings. For jurisdictions where there are six open seats spots, data shows that voters will fill in about 5.0 votes out of 6.0. It is common for voters not to know or not be pleased with a full list, and in those instances, as a voter, you reserve the right to vote for less than a full ballot. You reserve the right to leave some voting positions blank or to spoil your ballot. These are all democratic choices in Canada and different voters, for different reasons choose the approach that is right for them.

There is also some data that has been reported that suggests where a candidate is situated on a ballot may also have a minor impact on the voting patterns. In other words, all else being equal, a last name beginning with the letter "A" will garner more votes than a last name beginning with a "Z" if the ballots are prepared alphabetically. While there is nothing that an unelected candidate can do about this, there are some jurisdictions that have their ballots printed randomly so that there is a scrambling of names that occurs as ballots are printed. Once elected, this may be an example of legislation that an elected official can explore. But on Election Day it does not matter.

It is "gameday."

10.10 THE DAY AFTER ELECTION DAY

There may be bills to pay, family that has been neglected, the visiting of a loved one that has been delayed or a trip to a hospital that has been delayed. It matters that you handle these duties.

You should have pre-arranged your cleanup team to ensure any lawn signs, office cleanup, street signs or other materials are handled swiftly. I have seen campaigns where the losing candidates simply fold up their tent and do not clean their offices out, do not take down their street signs or even say thank you to volunteers. These are all real concerns that occur following close or bitter losses. Plan accordingly so that your campaign completes its work thoroughly and professionally. The work leading up to the campaign should already have included this kind of planning.

There are reports of individuals who have become depressed, where they are not able to function well (or at all) following a defeat. If you are aware of someone for whom this is a real possibility, the stress, anxiety and mental health of that person matters more than any lawn sign or other matter that is imminent. Reaching out to family members matters in this case.

10.11 THE DAYS AFTER ELECTION DAY

Your family, volunteers and known supporters deserve your time, they deserve your thanks, they deserve your moment thinking about each of them and this needs to be perhaps your highest priority.

Yes, there is the swearing into your new role, orientation, signing documents and much, much more. The demands on your time may be overwhelming. You may have to catch a flight, do media interviews and return texts and phone calls and emails. The demands come from new colleagues, your new leader, premier, prime minister, chief, reeve or mayor. Someone is arranging something for you that you did not know you had to do. All of that is also important, but so are those who helped you get to that point. Remember them.

Now, back to your spreadsheets. Print them off. These are people. There are door knockers, lawn sign hosts, workers, donors and more. This team are more responsible for helping you become elected than the people who need you next. This all seems obvious but is more often forgotten as the excitement of the new challenge looms.

It is time to call, text, email, send cards, send thank-you notes and send newspaper acknowledgments of gratitude. Thank others and do it now. It is they who need your time and caring thoughts. The spreadsheets are not complete until you have done so.

In 1991, columnist Fred Bauer wrote an article in *Reader's Digest* entitled "The Power of a Note." That title itself describes a lot about the importance of doing something caring, and do not underestimate the power of a handwritten note to those who helped you become elected.

I recall the words of the hunter who picked me up on the roadside during hunting season once. While he shared that "once you pull the trigger, the fun is all over," to some degree it could not be more correct at times, and yet more wrong at times. Serving others through a publicly elected office is one of the most gratifying and highest callings that we may experience in life.

Perhaps it should be said, "The fun has just begun."

APPENDICES

A. ANNOUNCEMENT – ACTUAL WORD FOR WORD

Nolan Crouse - Mayoralty Candidate
Official Announcement

May 16, 2013

I am pleased to share with you personally and formally that I plan to seek re-election for my third term as St. Albert's mayor on October 21, 2013.

I have thoroughly enjoyed the past nine years on council and the last six years as mayor. Serving the community in this manner is one of the most challenging and rewarding ways that a person can help make a difference, and I am grateful to the voters of St. Albert for having provided that opportunity to me. It is a sincere privilege to represent the city and the community of St. Albert.

I would like to thank the many people who have been supportive of me over the last several years. Specifically, my family and friends, fellow council members, the business community, City staff, campaign supporters, the media and the many volunteers, community clubs, organizations and groups who work tirelessly to build this thriving community. All of you allow me to assist in my way to help our city grow stronger and enrich all our lives.

My new election website will be launched later today at www.nolancrouse.com and summarizes my key platform priorities. A detailed platform of important matters will be posted later this summer, likely in September.

I will reserve any details on what I see as the 2014–2017 priorities until closer to the election so as not to unduly influence the important work that we have remaining on this council's term. Council has a very full agenda right up until our term ends at the October 21st election date.

Over the next few months, I will be requesting assistance of my family, friends, volunteers and supporters to assist in building a campaign team.

Thank you once again for your support and I ask that you continue to put your trust in me. All the best to you in the remainder of 2013, and please feel free to forward this message to anyone.

Nolan Crouse

Candidate for St. Albert Mayor 2013

Phone	555 555 5678
Email	nolanc@telusplanet.net
Website	www.nolancrouse.com
Blog	http://stalbertmayor.wordpress.com
	www.twitter.com/stalbertmayor
	www.facebook.com/nolancrouse9

B. SPEECH AT A TELEVISION DEBATE – ACTUAL WORD FOR WORD

Shaw Speech: September 28, 2010

To everyone here and those listening or watching at home.

My name is Nolan Crouse.

I am seeking the re-election to the Mayor's Chair for St. Albert.

I thank Shaw for this, and the moderators and volunteers for their work.

After six years on council, I would like to share where I see the key issues are for future improvement.

I have clearly heard that most love St. Albert and we must strengthen our social, environmental and economic areas.

What I hear the most is that the biggest challenge we face is keeping the tax structure affordable and sustainable.

Influencing the residential tax trend requires that we attract more commercial and industrial development.

Plans must include:

- supporting Downtown,
- further developing our Riel Business Park,
- solidifying plans for development North and West,
- completing the buildout of Campbell Park, and
- continuing to remove barriers to nurture a more business-friendly culture in the corporation and the community.

Secondly, I hear we must strengthen our sense of community.

Move forward on such things as

- community safety and community development;
- supporting our youth, seniors and persons with disabilities;
- ensuring a wider spectrum of affordable housing options are available for all; and
- putting in place a better process for public engagement in matters that affect us.

Third, environmentally, we will continue to reduce material going to landfill with the implementation of organic waste pickup. Plus, we need to find solutions to the state of the Sturgeon River Watershed.

Finally, guiding these fundamentals are the approaches we must use to bring it all together. Specifically, being a cooperative leader is required on regional and local matters.

To everyone, I am a businessman first and an experienced professional in both private and public companies, having managed two separate corporations larger than our City. And I have always served tirelessly and given to the communities we have lived in.

If re-elected, I will continue to serve with honour, respect, dignity and integrity.

I will engage Council, City staff, the community, the region and the province.

My name is Nolan Crouse.

C. POST-ELECTION LAWN SIGN INSTRUCTIONS
– ACTUAL WORD FOR WORD

Thank you very much for allowing your yard to host a lawn sign in support of my bid for re-election. We have taken care to install it in a good location, but feel free to move it as you see fit.

After the election, a crew will return to pick it up. Please leave it leaning against the side of your house and we will take it away the week after the election.

Please feel free to email me if you have campaign questions or need any matter addressed.

Again, thank you very much.

In the meantime, please spread the word about the election on October 21, and we need to encourage everyone to get out and vote.

Nolan Crouse

Candidate for Mayor, 2013

Phone	780 459 6899
Email	nolanc@telusplanet.net
Blog	http://stalbertmayor.wordpress.com
Website	www.nolancrouse.com

D. SAMPLE SPEECH – ACTUAL WORD FOR WORD

Chamber of Commerce Live Forum: October 15, 2013

Moderators
Organizers
To the Chamber

Candidates
Ladies and Gentlemen
My name is Nolan Crouse.

And I am seeking re-election to the Mayor's Chair for the City of St. Albert.

Thank you for this opportunity.

What I will share is a bit about myself but most importantly share what the key opportunities are that St. Albert faces.

For those who are perhaps new to St. Albert, I have been on Council for nine years, the last six years as mayor. I am a 59-year-old Alberta farm boy with a wife, Gwen, and three adult children, all living in St. Albert.

A NAIT Chemistry grad and an MBA in community economic development from Cape Breton University rounds out my education.

30 years in forest products, paralleled by 30 years coaching hockey is where I spent a lot of my time.

I will frame my thoughts around five priorities:
(5 FINGERS UP)

1. Long-term planning
2. Community development
3. Crime reduction
4. Business attraction
5. Age-friendly plan

First, we need to plan for this community's next two generations and as such, the first element of my platform is "Toward 200 planning" - planning for when we are 200 years old – only 48 more years.

Second, community development.
This means nurturing more new youth groups and continue supporting community groups in the future as we have in the past. Examples looking back include supporting Arts and Heritage Foundation activities, families rebuilding playgrounds and the community cleanup initiatives.

Our sense of community must be strengthened by better supporting young people, individuals in need, seniors in difficulty and persons with disabilities. This includes working with various community and advisory groups.

Third, to further solidify our position in Canada.
#1 place to live,

#1 place to raise a family,
#1 safest community rankings,

I am looking for Council's support to implement even more assertive programs with respect to crime.

Relative to crime,

- Knowing and communicating what the top 5 crime areas are
- Knowing what the top 5 crime issues are
- Knowing the police have priorities to address the top 5 groups or individuals involved in community crime

We must be relentless in pursuit of that sense of community safety, and I am calling that 5-5-5 strategy.

We live in a great city and cannot compromise the lifestyle values that provides us our sense of security. We must be relentless in pursuit of that security through this safety initiative.

- #4 is simply to crystallize the plans for non-residential development west of Ray Gibbon Drive 6-700 acres of light industrial. Working with the landowners who wish to sell.
- Working with the developers who are prepared to develop.
- Additionally, support the landowners to complete the buildout of Campbell Business Park, Riel Business Park and continue to support development of the commercial corridor north on the Trail.

Those are all key to our next phases of economic development and ultimately residential tax relief.

Finally, #5...develop a plan that transcends all ages, and to put in place a plan that is called an Age-Friendly Strategy.

This is becoming popular in communities, and we need to assess matters that are age sensitive such as making our Handi-bus trial successful into Edmonton, addressing mobility issues for seniors and to ensure there are more home options for downsizers and first-time buyers.

There are also important matters such as the 50+ Club new building rebuild, Sturgeon River health, Capital Region and Sturgeon County Regional work and other important local issues. Those are all listed on my blog and website.

How?

Being a cooperative leader is required on regional planning such as environmental activities, transportation and land planning, and economic development.

City Council will be expected to work with residents, with community groups, and within the region, and engage our outstanding City staff along the way.

To my fellow residents, I am a past businessperson and have been a professional for both private companies and public companies.

My wife and I have served on countless boards and have always given to the communities we have lived in.

I serve with honour.
I serve with dignity.
I serve with compassion.
I serve with integrity without exception.
I engage Council.
I engage the community.
I engage City staff.
I am a cooperative leader at the regional table of planning our future – protecting St. Albert, yet working for the greater good of the region and Alberta.
I will exhaust myself in pursuit of commercial and light industrial development.

Let me take you away for a minute...
Take you to construction zone.
Imagine these visuals:

- Construction around the casino lands
- Construction north of Costco
- Construction north of The Home Depot
- Construction west of Walmart
- Construction around The Enjoy Centre
- Construction west of Ray Gibbon Drive

You are going to see all that within the next 1to 4 years.

You know, to be the mayor requires one to have ability and experience.

The ability to paint those types of pictures of the future and to have the ability to work with others to see those same pictures, make them even better and implement plans to support them.

I humbly ask for your vote October 21st.

Again, my name is Nolan Crouse.

E. POST-ELECTION THANK YOU – ACTUAL WORD FOR WORD IN THE LOCAL NEWSPAPER

MAYOR SAYS THANKS

A heartfelt thank you!

To my fellow St. Albertans:

I wish to express my sincere thanks to my fellow St. Albertans for putting your trust in me to serve as your mayor for the next four years.

With serving in this capacity comes great responsibility, and I am certainly accepting the challenge of the honour entrusted to me. I take it seriously and you will always know that I do, because I care about the community of St. Albert and I care about the people of St. Albert.

I look forward to working with your new Council, with the community, its many businesses, our residents, the City staff, the region and the province as we look to build an even better St. Albert for everyone.

To my volunteers, donors and lawn sign hosts over the past few weeks, I thank you immensely. These extra attention to matters cannot be done without your support.

Finally, to my family and those closest to me, I offer a special thank you as it is in these times when we know just how important it is to come together for one another.

As always, I will see you out and about in the community.

Mayor, Nolan Crouse

F. LETTER TO DONORS – ACTUAL WORD FOR WORD

[Date]

[Company]

This is to express my sincere gratitude and thanks to you and your company for providing support of me for the Mayor Campaign in St. Albert where I was seeking to be re-elected.

With support such as what you were able to provide, it allowed me the opportunity to share with others the important matters that face our community in the years ahead. These matters include growth-related infrastructure, diversifying the tax base through business attraction and planning, working to attract young families and planning for an aging community (both aging infrastructure and an aging population).

There is always much to do, and I am appreciative that I have been given the opportunity to help serve the community once again in the role as St. Albert's Mayor. It is with your generous support that I was able to do that and for that I am appreciative.

All the best
Yours truly,

Nolan Crouse

Nolan Crouse
Mayor, City of St. Albert
The Botanical Arts City

Lightning Source UK Ltd.
Milton Keynes UK
UKHW020749140721
387106UK00007B/123